GPS – God's Positioning System:

Locating God's Plan and Purpose for Your Life

By Jide Lawore

Dedication

This book is dedicated to the many servants of God who have abundantly contributed to my spiritual understanding, knowledge, and development over the years. I am a product of their sacrifice and labor in the Word of God. What you are about to read is in large part due to the impact these heroes have made upon my life. Over the past twenty years I have listened to their messages, read their works, and observed their lives. Now I am standing on their shoulders and passing forward the torch of knowledge. To all the great saints who have helped mold my life and ministry, I thankfully dedicate this book.

Table of Contents

Acknowledgments

This book is a product of lifelong learning from many teachers, mentors, and fathers in the faith. They are too many for me to mention, but I want to say of them that I am indebted to your labor of love and your investment, and for this I thank you.

Just like in any sport, writing is a team effort. I want to acknowledge people who have contributed to the successful completion of this book. First, my church family, Agape House of Worship. This work began as a message series in Agape House, and the feedback and testimonies I received from many of you provided the encouragement to write this book.

I also want to say a special thanks to my dad, Pa Timothy Lawore, a retired school principal who is also now in full-time ministry. He instilled in me a culture of reading from a very young age that has helped me greatly in life and in ministry. Also, as God would have it, he happened to be visiting with me in the United States toward the completion of this book. He took time to read through the manuscript and provided critical inputs.

Finally, I want to acknowledge my wife, Abimbola Lawore, who has been my greatest cheerleader, supporter, and partner in ministry. Your encouragement, push, and unwavering support played a great role in my getting the courage to start writing this book.

Introduction

The Global Positioning System (GPS) is a navigation and precise-positioning tool developed by the Department of Defense in 1973. It was originally designed to assist soldiers in accurately determining the locations of their military vehicles, planes, and ships worldwide. Today, the uses of GPS have extended to include both the commercial and scientific worlds. Commercially, GPS is used as a navigation and positioning tool in airplanes, boats, cars, and for almost all outdoor recreational activities such as hiking, fishing, and kayaking. In the scientific community, GPS plays an important role in the earth sciences. Meteorologists use it for weather forecasting and global climate studies, and geologists can use it as a highly accurate method of surveying and in earthquake studies to measure tectonic motions during and in between earthquakes.

GPS devices, whether built into a car or phone or as a handheld device, have revolutionized the way we travel, especially in America and the rest of the developed world. Chances are you have GPS in your car or phone or have a handheld device. It is a big improvement from the days of the paper map or even directions from MapQuest.

This book talks about a GPS, but not the one in your car or your smart phone. It is about a higher kind of GPS. It is called God's Positioning System. Just as the GPS Global Positioning System guides you and gives you directions when you drive or hike, God also has a plan to guide his children though the roads of life. His plan for us is not to go through life mumbling and fumbling around. No, he has a plan and purpose for your life, and he has provided a way for you to know it.

The goal of this book is to challenge, encourage, guide, and teach you to embrace God's plan and purpose for your life and to find out how you can be positioned in his plan. God said to Jeremiah, "For I know the plans I have for you . . . plans to prosper you and not to harm you, plans to give you hope and a future" (Jeremiah 29:11). Paul prayed for the Ephesians, "that the eyes of your heart may be enlightened in order that you may know the hope to which he has called you, the riches of his glorious inheritance in his holy people"(Ephesians 1:18). The good news is that not only does God have a plan; he wants us to know the plan. The goal of this book is to show you how you can know and enter into God's glorious plan for your life. That is what the Christian life is all about, and I pray this book will help you to begin that journey of purpose that will lead you to your inheritance in Christ Jesus. Amen.

Chapter 1

Lost?

The spirit of a man is the lamp of the Lord, searching
all the inner depths of his heart.

— Proverbs 20:27 NKJV

Apart from the assurance of your eternal destination,
one of the greatest benefits of being a believer in Christ
Jesus is your ability to know God's plan for your life. This
ability to know God's mind concerning you, to understand
his ways, to figure out what he is doing in your life and what
he wants you to do, is crucial to your success and the quality
of your life. This is what creates a life of confidence, purpose,
joy, and fulfillment. Unfortunately, many believers, unaware
of these benefits, live a life of confusion, devoid of direction,
and tossed to and fro by life's situations and circumstances.

I want to start by letting you know that it is not God's will
that any of his children live in confusion. Confusion is a function of darkness, and darkness represents everything that is of
the devil. That is why the Bible calls the kingdom of the devil
the "kingdom of darkness." The kingdom of God, however,
is called light. Light represents clarity, the ability to see and
understand what is going on around you and what lies ahead.
In the book of Genesis, one of the first things God did after the
creation of the heaven and the earth was to create light.

Now the earth was formless and empty, darkness was
over the surface of the deep, and the Spirit of God was
hovering over the waters.

13

And God said, "Let there be light," and there was light. God saw that the light was good, and he separated the light from the darkness. God called the light "day," and the darkness he called "night." And there was evening, and there was morning — the first day.

—Genesis 1:2–5

Notice what the scripture says here; the earth was formless, empty, and darkness was all over the place. As long as there is darkness, there is formlessness, emptiness, confusion, and disorder. God changed all that and instituted order by first of all creating light. It was after light was created that he then proceeded with the rest of the creation. Also notice that God did not declare anything good until light came; it was actually light that brought beauty to the rest of the creation. Nothing good comes out of darkness. Anywhere there is darkness there is ugliness, for it is light that brings beauty. In the spiritual sense, this is what happens when Christ comes into any life. When Christ comes, light comes. In fact the Bible says that he himself is light.

In him was life, and that life was the light of all mankind. The light shines in the darkness, and the darkness has not overcome it.

—John 1:4–5

When you accept Jesus Christ as your Lord and Savior, light comes to your heart. You are introduced to the light and given a perpetual access to light. As you continue to follow him, that light then becomes your way of life.

For with you is the fountain of life; in your light we see light.

—Psalm 36:9

Confusion Is Not God's Plan for You

Unfortunately many believers in Christ Jesus still live in darkness and confusion. This ought not to be so. We are not

14

of darkness but of light. The bible clearly says we have been rescued from the kingdom of darkness and translated into the kingdom of light (see Colossians 1:13). Anywhere there is darkness there is confusion, chaos, and misunderstanding. On the other hand, anywhere there is light there is clarity, order, and understanding. Anywhere the Spirit of God is there is no confusion because God is not the author of confusion. If you are living in confusion, I want to assure you that it is not God's plan for you. In Christ Jesus God has made provision for light for his children.

> But you, brothers and sisters, are not in darkness so that this day should surprise you like a thief. You are all children of the light and children of the day. We do not belong to the night or to the darkness. So then, let us not be like others, who are asleep, but let us be awake and sober.

> —1 Thessalonians 5:4–6

When you are living in darkness you are lost; you are surrounded with uncertainties, lack of assurance, doubt, and ignorance. These are not attributes of God's kingdom or of the children of the kingdom. If you are a child of God and still live in confusion, doubt, and fear, I want to challenge you that this is not God's plan for you. You have been rescued from the kingdom of darkness and translated into the kingdom of light. Ignorance of this fact is responsible in many ways for weakness and exploitation of many believers by the enemy. The enemy wants to keep you in ignorance and in darkness of who you are in Christ and the provision God has made for you in Christ Jesus. I am trusting God that this book will challenge you to rise up from your slumber and embrace God's light.

Naturally Lost

There are two reasons why a person can be lost spiritually. The primary reason is lack of relationship with Christ. According to the Word of God, people without Christ are lost. Without Christ man is lost, with no sense of direction and purpose. Jesus Christ is the only way to God (see John 14:6); every other way will lead to a wrong destination. The only way to find God's plan and destination for your life is through Christ. Outside of Christ there is no purpose and fulfillment. It is clear from the Scripture, regardless of who you are and how you are born, you are not a product of accident—God created you for his pleasure and purpose. You are a deliberate and carefully planned creation of God. When God made man in the Garden of Eden, it was a deliberate act. He told the host of heaven, "Let us make man in our image, after our likeness" (Genesis 1:26 KJV). You were meant to be like God.

When Adam and Eve sinned, the whole plan was thwarted, at least temporarily. Man was eternally separated from God and hence from God's plan and purpose for him. When God told Adam, "But of the tree of the knowledge of good and evil you shall not eat, for in the day that you eat of it you shall surely die" (Genesis 2:17 NKJV), what he meant was spiritual death. In a broader sense, death means separation. Physical death means separation of the human spirit from the physical body, and spiritual death means separation of the human spirit from God. That is what happened to Adam and Eve and by extension the whole human race. The day Adam and Eve ate from the tree of knowledge of good and evil, we all died spiritually.

So when the Bible says in 1 Corinthians 15:22, "For as in Adam all die, so in Christ all will be made alive," the Bible is simply saying that through the sin of Adam the whole human race became separated from God, and through Christ Jesus we all became reunited with God. Every person born of a woman is born into a state of spiritual death (see Ephesians 2:1), with the spirit separated from God and unable to communicate with him. That is why without Jesus Christ man will just be wandering around aimlessly with no purpose and clear destination.

In the book of 1 Thessalonians, the inspired writer Paul revealed that man has a triune nature that consists of the spirit, the soul, and the body (see 5:23). Of the three components, the only one that can relate with God is the spirit. It is with our spirit that we can connect to God. God is Spirit, therefore he sees man primarily as a spirit.

> The spirit of a man is the lamp of the Lord, searching all the inner depths of his heart.
>
> —Proverbs 20:27 NKJV

> God is spirit, and his worshipers must worship in the Spirit and in truth.
>
> —John 4:24

From the scriptures above it's clear that your spirit is the lamp of the Lord—it is God's gateway to you. That is the part of you that concerns God the most. You worship God in your spirit. Without the spirit, worship and, in fact, relationship with God is impossible. When God wants to speak to you he speaks to your spirit, not to your mind or body. Your spirit then translates God's message to your mind and your mind to your body. That is how man was originally designed to function. That is also why an unsaved man is eternally lost; his spirit is incapable of knowing God, hearing God, worshipping God, and fellowshipping with God. He is eternally separated from God.

In 1 Corinthians chapters 2 and 3, Apostle Paul describes three kinds of man based on our spiritual status: the natural man, the carnal man, and the spiritual man. The natural man is the unsaved or unregenerate man. Here is how he describes the natural man:

> But the natural man does not receive the things of the Spirit of God, for they are foolishness to him; nor can he know them, because they are spiritually discerned. But he who is spiritual judges all things, yet he himself is rightly judged by no one.
>
> —1 Corinthians 2:14–15 NKJV

We have already said that man was designed to relate and communicate with God by his spirit; but the spirit of an unsaved man is dead. He is dead to God and cannot receive from God.

Because the spirit is dead the natural man is therefore controlled by his soul, which consists of his mind, will, and emotions. However the unregenerate soul is incapable of pleasing God. The spiritual man is a man that functions the way God intended. The spirit is alive and in control, he is therefore a spirit-controlled man. Let us look at some of the characteristics of the natural man in the Scriptures:

- *The natural man is separated from God.* The natural man cannot have a personal relationship with God. Relationship by nature involves communication and fellowship. A natural man is incapable of doing all that because he is dead to God. We have earlier said that the spirit of man in his natural state is dead to God. Hence unless the spirit is made alive through Christ the natural man cannot have a relationship with God no matter how he tries. Also, when a natural man dies his spirit is eternally dead and becomes eternally separated from God in hell. Hell is a place of torment and eternal separation from God.

- *The natural man is dead in trespasses and sin.* The bible says: "As for you, you were dead in your transgressions and sins, in which you used to live when you followed the ways of this world and of the ruler of the kingdom of the air, the spirit who is now at work in those who are disobedient" (Ephesians 2:1–2). When the bible says the natural man is dead in sin and trespasses, it means he is lost in sin, insensitive to sin, and incapable of knowing that he is living in sin. The conscience of an unsaved man is dead to sin; hence he is incapable of living a life of obedience to God.

- *The natural man is under the control of the rulers of the kingdom of the air.* Ephesians 2:1–2 also states that the natural man is under the control of the kingdom of the air. This means he is under the control of the forces of evil and demonic spirits. Jesus also called the devil "the prince of this world" (John 14:30), that means to a large

extent the devil controls the world system and everything in it. If you are unsaved you are at the mercy of the
demonic spirits. This is because the power over demons
can only come from God and that power can only be
communicated by the Spirit of God into your spirit. This
is impossible for the natural man because the spirit of the
natural man is dead to God. When Christ died and rose
from the dead, he defeated the power of darkness and
handed over the victory to those who believe in him.

- *The natural man is naturally disobedient to God.*
Inside the natural man is the spirit of disobedience
(see Ephesians 2:2). The word translated "spirit" here
really means an attitude, a mental disposition, or a
nature. This means that inside of him, the natural
man has a mental disposition to live in disobedience
to God. Romans 8:8 says: "Those controlled by the
sinful nature cannot please God." The sinful nature is
the fallen human soul, which is naturally disposed to
please itself not God. It is an attitude to be the boss and
ignore God's principles for living.

- *The natural man is unable to hear God.* Because he is
dead to God, the natural man cannot hear God. God
speaks to man through the human spirit. The Scripture
says, "The Spirit himself testifies with our spirit that
we are God's children" (Romans 8:16). The Holy Spirit
speaks to our spirit to attest and affirm that we are
children of God. It is that ability to hear God's voice
that makes us children of God. "And because you are
sons, God has sent forth the Spirit of His Son into your
hearts, crying out, 'Abba, Father!' Therefore you are no
longer a slave but a son, and if a son, then an heir of
God through Christ" (Galatians 4:6–7 NKJV).

- *The natural man is blind to the gospel.* The spiritual eye
of the natural man is blind and cannot see the light of
God, which is the gospel. The Bible says, "The god of this
age has blinded the minds of unbelievers, so that they

cannot see the light of the gospel that displays the glory of Christ, who is the image of God." (2 Corinthians 4:4). Therefore the natural man is perpetually lost until Jesus Christ, the light of the world, comes into his life. That is why the gospel doesn't make sense to an unbeliever; it takes a conviction of the Holy Spirit for a person to be saved. Sometimes as believers we argue with unbelievers over spiritual stuff as if they might really understand it. No, they don't, and what we need to do for the unsaved is pray that they will be convicted by the Holy Spirit.

As mentioned eailier, if the natural man is a man whose spirit is dead and separated from God, the spiritual man is a man whose spirit is alive and united with God.

But he who is spiritual judges all things, yet he himself is rightly judged by no one.

—1 Corinthians 2:15 NKJV

When we accept Jesus as our Lord and Savior, our dead spirit is regenerated and made alive in Christ Jesus. The Bible says, "And you He made alive, who were dead in trespasses and sins" (Ephesians 2:1 NKJV). However becoming saved does not necessarily make us spiritual, becoming spiritual involves a long process of spiritual growth and maturity.

Saved but Still Lost

The secondary reason why a man can be lost spiritually is what Apostle Paul calls carnality. This is how Apostle Paul describes the carnal man:

And I, brethren, could not speak to you as to spiritual people but as to carnal, as to babes in Christ. I fed you with milk and not with solid food; for until now you were not able to receive it, and even now you are still not able; for you are still carnal. For where there are envy, strife, and divisions among you, are you not carnal and behaving like mere men?

—1 Corinthians 3:1–3 NKJV

20

The natural man is an unsaved man whose spirit is dead and is primarily controlled by his mind. The spiritual man is a man whose spirit is alive and who is controlled by his spirit, which is in turn controlled by the Holy Spirit. A carnal man, however, is a saved man who is still largely controlled by the soul. For the carnal man, the spirit is alive but weak and incapable of control. For the spirit to be in control it has to first be made alive through salvation and second be made strong through spiritual edification. That is why Apostle Paul prayed for the Ephesian church, "That out of his glorious riches he may strengthen you with power through his Spirit in your inner being" (Ephesians 3:16). Your inner being is your spirit. He also told the Corinthian church that "he who speaks in a tongue edifies himself" (1 Corinthians 14:4 NKJV). To edify means to improve or build up. Because the spirit is weak, the carnal man finds himself constantly fluctuating between being spirit controlled and soul controlled. Let us look at some of the characteristics of the carnal man.

- *The carnal man is spiritually immature.* One of the key attributes of the carnal man is immaturity; this is due to a lack of solid food of the Word of God. Even though the spirit is alive, it needs to be fed with the Word of God so it can be healthy enough to communicate with God and overcome the control of the soul. Paul chastised the Corinthian church for not wanting to grow up in the spirit by refusing the food of the Spirit. Apostle Peter also admonished the believers: "Like newborn babies, crave pure spiritual milk, so that by it you may grow up in your salvation" (1 Peter 2:2).The growth they were both talking about is the growth of the spirit man. It is the human spirit that is reborn and needs to grow. Carnality is immaturity, and it the natural product of a lack of spiritual growth.

- *The carnal man practically lives like the natural man.* Though he is saved and the spirit is alive, the carnal man yields more to the dictate of the flesh (which is another Bible name for the soul) than to that of the spirit. This makes the quality of the life of a carnal man little different from that of the natural man. That is why Apostle Paul accuses the Corinthians of behaving like mere men. By mere men he meant natural man, without Christ and the Holy Spirit.

For you are still carnal. For where there are envy, strife, and divisions among you, are you not carnal and behaving like mere men?

—1 Corinthians 3:3 NKJV

• *The carnal man lives with a constant battle between his spirit and soul.* Another name for the human soul is "sinful nature." It is in the soul that our sinful tendency resides. In Genesis 2:17, the tree of sin that Adam and Eve ate from is called "tree of the knowledge of good and evil." The eating from this tree led to consciousness of sin and tendency to sin, which reside in the soul. When a man gets saved, the human spirit becomes injected with the life of God. This automatically leads to a battle for control between the human spirit and the soul. The soul, which had been used to being in control, does not want to yield the control to the spirit, who is now the new boss. But because the spirit of the carnal man is weak, he constantly lives in tension and defeat.

For the sinful nature desires what is contrary to the Spirit, and the Spirit what is contrary to the sinful nature. They are in conflict with each other, so that you do not do what you want.

—Galatians 5:17 NKJV

• *The carnal man has no sense of direction or purpose.* Because the spirit of the carnal man is weak it is unable to have a dynamic and effective relationship with God. The human spirit is the GPS receiver that receives the signals from the spiritual satellites. Our spiritual satellite is God through the Holy Spirit. Hence, because of the weakness of the spirit, the carnal man constantly struggles and unsure when it comes to God's purpose and direction.

The human spirit is the lamp of the Lord that sheds light on one's inmost being.

—Proverbs 20:27

In the GPS world, the quality of the signal received depends on the quality of the GPS receiver. Some receivers take forever to acquire signals from the satellites. Such a GPS unit gives its owner a lot of frustrations when traveling, and sometimes they are not worth the money. That is why it is always better to spend a little more to buy a quality GPS receiver, because it saves you a lot of frustration. The interesting thing is that the signal is the same — the satellites do not send a weak signal to some receivers and a strong signal to others. The quality of your signal is determined only by the quality of your GPS receiver.

This is also applicable in the spiritual world. The quality of your spirit (in terms of how much you edify, strengthen, and feed your spirit) determines the quality of the signal you receive from God. Hence the carnal man is also constantly lost, mumbling and fumbling through life because he is unable to clearly hear God and understand the message God is sending.

Unfortunately this is the condition of many believers today; the spirit is alive because we are saved but weak because it is not being edified. We are saved but immature. Hence, we are constantly lost, confused, and unable to understand God's plan and purpose for our lives. The responsibility to develop our spirit primarily lies on us. God will help us, but we must take the initiative. Just like Apostle Paul prayed for the Ephesians, we must pray that God will strengthen our inner man through the Holy Spirit; we must feed our spirit with the Word of God (see 1 Peter 2:2), we must pray without ceasing both in understanding and in the spirit (see 1 Corinthians 14:4, Jude v. 20), and we must train and exercise our spirit toward godliness (see 1 Timothy 4:8). It is in doing all these that we can make our spirit strong, healthy, and capable of fellowshipping and communing with God and hearing from God effectively. It is my sincere prayer that God will use this book to aid you in doing just that in Jesus' name.

Chapter 2

God's GPS

Whether you turn to the right or to the left, your ears will hear a voice behind you, saying, "This is the way; walk in it."

—Isaiah 30:21

C hances are that you drive a car equipped with a navigation system (commonly called GPS), or you have a handheld GPS device or a smart phone that comes with GPS. Even if you don't, I want to assume that at least you know someone who does. The GPS navigation system serves as a good location finder when you are lost or trying to make your way through busy streets. The GPS navigation system replaces a map while still maintaining its main purpose, to give direction. This system makes driving easier, faster, and more enjoyable. You don't have to read those complicated maps while you are trying to drive. You don't have to argue with the person sitting next to you about whether you go left, right, or make a U-turn. You don't have to stop and ask for directions. And you don't have to loose focus on your driving. The GPS navigation has eliminated all these hassles that a conventional map can cause.

The GPS technology is one of the wonderful inventions of our time. Have you ever thought about how we got directions before the invention of GPS? Many years ago, if you wanted to visit someone, you simply called and they give you detailed directions. They'd tell you for example, "Take exit ten on the highway and make a right after the ramp. After driving for about one mile, make a right, there is a Wal-Mart at that corner; then continue to drive five minutes, and you will see a Shell gas station on your right. When you drive a little bit farther, just about five miles, you are going to see a 7-Eleven. The road after 7-Eleven is called King Street; make a right on King Street. After that, make the first left, onto Dora Street."

Do you remember those days? That is how typical directions used to sound. Some people were good at using maps. Have you ever seen someone park their car on the side of the road and bring out a map to try to find their way around? Then came the Internet age, and thanks to MapQuest and Yahoo, we graduated to using customized printed directions. You simply put in a start and end address and you are able to generate step-by-step directions to your destination. So you have the printed directions in one hand and are driving with the other hand. The limitation of the directions becomes apparent when you miss your turn or you meet a roadblock due to an accident or construction. The directions become useless, so you either find your way back to that point where you got lost and try to trace it back again or you call your destination to get the old-fashioned verbal directions.

After all these came the Global Positioning System, which we call simply GPS, if you have ever used the GPS for direction while driving I am sure you will agree with me that it is something you can no longer do without. In fact, after driving with it for a while you start wondering how you survived without it. I remember the first time I got to use a GPS receiver; my wife and I were looking for a family car and we said, "Let's get a car that is 'fully loaded,' " and fully loaded for that particular car meant that it came with a navigation system. Driving the car and using the GPS for the first time was an amazing experience for me. You turn the system on, punch in your destination address, and it begins to guide you step-by-step, telling you where to go, when to turn left or right, and how long to travel on a particular road. When you get lost it has a function called "recalculate." It simply reconfigures your directions to the original destination from the new location. That first time was an amazing experience.

One of the beautiful things about GPS is that you don't care anymore about memorizing your directions or the important landmarks along the way. All you need is the destination address and your ability to follow simple instruction, and you are sure you will get to your destination. In fact, after about a month or so of driving my new car with the GPS, it became very difficult to drive our second car, which is without GPS. Sometimes I would forget and get into the car without the GPS and set out without any printed directions, and it would suddenly occur to me, "Oh no, I have no directions." I would either go back inside to print out directions or simply switch to the new car with the GPS.

After a few months of doing this we decided to go buy one of those handheld GPS devices. Thank God someone came up with the idea of a portable handheld GPS receiver and that they are relatively cheap to buy. So we went and got one of those and started using it with the other car. That is how I became totally dependent on GPS for getting around. Regardless of what you think of it, GPS has totally revolution-ized the way we travel.

It amazes me that some people still get their directions the old-fashioned way. A couple of years ago an older gentleman wanted to come and visit us. I was amazed when he called us and said, "Just give me the address. Where is your town? I will get there." Guess what happened? Two hours later, when he couldn't find our place, he got frustrated and went back to his house. He called later and said, "I couldn't locate the address. I stopped at several gas stations and people kept giving me different directions, so I got frustrated and went back home." I thought to myself, if this man continues to get lost in this manner, he will spend so much on gas alone that he could have bought a handheld GPS device.

I have gone through the trouble of relating my GPS con-version story to make a very important point: How about if we have a GPS for our life? As bad as getting lost is when we drive, it is not as bad as getting lost in our life's journey. Can you imagine if God had a GPS device for us that can actually guide us through life, so we know who to marry, where to live, and what career path to follow? The good news is that he does, and that is what this book is about. God actually has a GPS-like plan for our life. As a believer in Christ Jesus, it is not God's intention that you constantly get lost and confused as you go through life. It is also not his intention that you just keep getting direction from bystanders along the way. It is not his will that you live your life in confusion, without clarity, sense of direction, or a clear understanding of your destination. God has a plan of direction so that no believer or any person who is a child of God should ever live their lives without a clear direction and purpose.

If you are currently confused, directionless, and unsure, this book is written to encourage you and to show you that God has a plan for you. I will start by showing you what God has to say to us through the great prophet Jeremiah:

> "For I know the plans I have for you," declares the Lord, "plans to prosper you and not to harm you, plans to give you hope and a future."
>
> —Jeremiah 29:11

In my curiosity, I did a little research about how GPS works. I know some of you readers are probably more computer literate or more technologically advanced and will understand this better. What we call GPS is actually a GPS receiver. The Global Positioning System itself is a combination of so many objects called satellites. Satellites are objects that the United States military put into space to get signals. There are twenty-seven of these objects that are hanging up there in space. Each of these satellites is circling around the earth twice a day, so that at any point in time, regardless of where you are located, your receiver can connect to at least four of them. The four of them are visible to the receiver you are holding. They are getting signals; they are taking pictures of every location. Information about every location on the earth is conveyed by these satellites.

The United States military came up with this technology and was using it for their own purposes, which includes targeting enemy locations and things like that. Many years later the U.S. government decided to open it up for public and commercial use and benefit. One of the results is that we now have GPS receivers available for us to use virtually anywhere we go.

This is how the GPS works: Your receiver gets signals and the little computer inside the receiver will quickly perform some calculations. It is very interesting how these calculations are done. One satellite tells your system you are 90 miles north of this place, another satellite tells the system you are 60 miles or 100 miles east of this other place. . . . The receiver gets three or four of those signals, does the calculation, and then locates the exact position where you are on the surface of the earth—anywhere. Isn't it amazing how GPS works?

Let us now look into the Scripture and see what the Bible says about God's plan to guide and direct his children:

> Whether you turn to the right or to the left, your ears will hear a voice behind you, saying, "This is the way; walk in it."

> —Isaiah 30:21

God is the Creator of heaven and earth. The Bible says he makes known the end from the beginning (see Isaiah 46:10). When he called Prophet Jeremiah and Jeremiah was having trouble believing him because he thought he was unqualified, God told him, "Before I formed you in the womb I knew you." This is not only true about Jeremiah; it is also true about you. There is nothing about you that is new to him. He knew you before you were born, and he knew when you were going to be born, and he knows when you are going to die. He knows everything about you.

I'd like us to also read another scripture, from the book of Acts.

> From one man he made all the nations, that they should inhabit the whole earth; and he marked out their appointed times in history and the boundaries of their lands.

> — Acts 17:26

Look at that scripture; if you are a child of God looking for God's plan and purpose, this should give you a lot of encouragement. God has a plan and purpose for you. He determines when you are going to live. Some people lived in the nineteenth century; some people lived in the tenth century. God wants you to live in this twenty-first century; that is why you are living in now. That scripture also says that he determines the exact place you will live, too. God's plan for you is geographical. As a believer you don't just wake up one day and say, "I am tired of this place; I am moving to that place." You should learn to consult him and let him lead you the way you should go. God's plan for you is not random in nature; it is not just a hit or miss. It is specific and precise.

I remember this story vividly. I was back in Nigeria, and I had finished college and was doing what we called National Youth Service. In Nigeria after you graduate from college you must serve the country for one year, working for the government or wherever you are assigned in a different part of the country than where you are from. One of my good friends whom I met during the Youth Service came to me and asked me to pray with him so that God would open a door for him to travel to America. He is a firm believer in Christ, and we had spent a lot of time together fellowshipping and studying the Bible together. So this day he came to me and said, "I would like you to pray and fast together with me because my desire is to migrate to the United States after our Youth Service." He wanted us to spend some time to pray and fast together about the issue. So I said, "It's okay. That's what friends are there for."

Then we prayed and fasted. We fasted and prayed together for about three days. In the course of the fasting, I discovered Acts 17:26. I was just reading that scripture; it just popped up to me. So I went to my friend and said, "You know what? I was reading this scripture, and I never saw it like this before. I was just reading and stumbled upon it and there was an impression about this scripture that I got, which made me feel it is relevant to our prayer. Instead of just bombarding God about going to America, why don't we just ask God to locate us where he wants us to be? The Bible says he determines when we are going to live and he determines the boundaries of our habitation. I think our prayer should be, 'I don't want to cross that boundary; I want to be in your will.' "

The best place to be, always, is in the will of God. It gives you a life of peace and divine assurance. No matter what is happening to you, as long as you know you are in his will, you are immovable. You are unshakeable because you know his plans for you are good plans. They are perfect plans; you know he gives you a future and a hope. The good news here is not just that God has a plan; it is that we can find out what his plan is. That is what this book is about and I am sure that is probably why you chose to read this book. As you read this book it is my sincere prayer that you will have an encounter with God that will change your life for good in Jesus' name.

Chapter 3

Power of Promises

Through these he has given us his very great and precious promises, so that through them you may participate in the divine nature, having escaped the corruption in the world caused by evil desires.

—2 Peter 1:4

In this chapter and next we are going to look at God's promises as they relate to guiding his people. We will devote some time to looking at some of his promises concerning us in the area of guidance. This is important because everything about God starts with his promises. After going through these verses, I trust you will no longer have any excuse to say, "I don't know" or "I am confused." I will like to repeat it to you again that as a believer it is not God's intention for you to just muddle and jumble through life. It is not God's will for you to live your life by guessing. It is not God's will for you to live life just based on every thought and idea that comes to you. No. You have the promises from God to live by, and you can know what his plan for you is. I am speaking to you about God's Positioning System. At every point in time God positions every one of us, based on his plans and purposes. Here are few things to note about God and his promises:

1. Everything God does starts with a promise.

Everything with God starts with a promise—it is very important for you to know this—everything God wants to do in your life starts with a promise. He gives you promises and it is your responsibility to know and understand his promises. If you are a good student of the Bible, you will know that every great thing God did in the Bible was as a result of somebody who found a promise relating to a circumstance or challenge and then claimed the promise appropriately. This is a continuous theme in the Bible. Powerful prayers with powerful results in the Bible are prayers soundly based on the promise of God.

In the book of Genesis God made a promise to Abraham (see chapters 12-15). God told him, "You are going to have a child and that child is going to be a blessing to the whole world; through him the whole world will be blessed. That child is also going to have a child and at a point your descendants are going to go to Egypt and are going to be in bondage of slavery with the Egyptians for four hundred years. Then I am going to rescue them by my mighty hands and punish the nation that enslaved them." God told Abraham all this.

> Then the Lord said to him, "Know for certain that for four hundred years your descendants will be strangers in a country not their own and that they will be enslaved and mistreated there. But I will punish the nation they serve as slaves, and afterward they will come out with great possessions.
>
> —Genesis 15:13-14

Many years later, you will discover, everything happened just as the Lord told Abraham. Joseph, Abraham's great-grandson, went to Egypt as part of God's plan. His own brothers, moved by jealousy and hatred, sold him into slavery, and he found himself in the house of Potiphar, who was an official in Egypt. From there he landed in prison as a victim of Potiphar's wife's wickedness. By God's divine providence and arrangement, God moved Joseph from prison to become the Prime Minister of Egypt and second in command to the King Pharaoh himself. Meanwhile there was famine in the whole region, which led Isaac, Joseph's father, and his brothers (who sold him to slavery) to find themselves in Egypt. They were forced to confront their past wickedness and apologized to

Joseph. The whole family, and hence descendants of Abraham, eventually made Egypt their home. After many years and many generations in Egypt, the king that knew Joseph died and the Israelites became slaves for over four hundred years.

When they were close to four hundred years in Egypt, some Israelites, being aware of God's promise, began to say among themselves, "This suffering is too much, and I think it is time for us to leave this place. We have a promise through our father Abraham." The Bible says the children of Israel began to pray. In Exodus chapter 3, it says they cried unto the Lord and the Lord hearkened unto them and God raised Moses the prophet and the deliverer. After many encounters with Pharaoh and miraculous manifestations of God's power, the children of Israel were delivered from the hand of the Egyptians, and the Egyptians were punished according to the promise of God to Abraham.

In the same manner God told the children of Israel through Prophet Jeremiah, "You are going to be taken into captivity by the Babylonians and you are going to be there for seventy years. And after seventy years I will rescue you" (see Jeremiah 25:9–12). They were in captivity, truly according to the word of the Lord, until one man, Daniel, was reading the book of Jeremiah and discovered God's promise and said, "Wow! We are supposed to be here for seventy years. The seventieth year is approaching. I have to do something about it." The Bible says Daniel went fasting. He began to pray and said, "God, this is your promise. You said seventy years and I am claiming seventy years." And the children of Israel were delivered.

> In the first year of Darius son of Xerxes (a Mede by descent), who was made ruler over the Babylonian kingdom — in the first year of his reign, I, Daniel, understood from the Scriptures, according to the word of the Lord given to Jeremiah the prophet, that the desolation of Jerusalem would last seventy years. So I turned to the Lord God and pleaded with him in prayer and petition, in fasting, and in sackcloth and ashes.
>
> — Daniel 9:1–3

This is the point of these stories: Everything God is going to do in your life will originate from your understanding God's promises for your life. Look at how the Bible puts it: "Daniel understood from the Scriptures." How did he understand? It is by studying the Scriptures. In fact, the Contemporary English Version puts it this way: "I found out from studying the writings of the prophets."

To back up what I am saying, I would like to show you another important scripture written by the great apostle Peter.

> His divine power has given us everything we need for a godly life through our knowledge of him who called us by his own glory and goodness. Through these he has given us his very great and precious promises, so that through them you may participate in the divine nature, having escaped the corruption in the world caused by evil desires.
>
> —2 Peter 1:3–4

There is a corruption in the world. I don't think that needs a lot of explanation. If you have lived a few years on earth you know that the world we are in is indeed very corrupted. The good news is that as believers God wants us to escape that corruption. He doesn't want us to be part of the corruption; he doesn't want us to partake in the mess that is going on. To achieve this he has given us his exceeding great and precious promises. It is through these promises that we can escape the corruption that is the world. We are all trapped in this evil thing called the world, but he says you can escape that evil, and the way to escape is through the promises that have been given to you. So God's promises are very important.

2. You must know God's promises.

God has given us everything we need through his promises. In order to enjoy his divine nature we must know the promises. In response to the temptation of the devil, Jesus told us: "It is written: 'Man shall not live on bread alone, but on every word that comes from the mouth of God' " (Matthew

4:4). You must live by the Word; that is very important. You live by the promises; you escape the corruption that is in the word through the promises. Daniel found out God's promises from studying the writings of the prophets, and that led to a powerful prayer that altered the course of a nation. The Israelites discovered God's promise to their father Abraham, and that lead to a great cry that earned them respect from God.

The big question is, how many of those promises do you know? How many of those promises do you claim? In your prayers, how many times do you go to God and tell him, "God, this is your promise. I am holding unto you." I have discovered that many times when believers pray, we just pray our emotions. Unfortunately God is not moved by your emotions. God is not moved by your cry based on your emotions. You can't just cry and expect God to do something because of your cry. Human beings can do something for you because you cried — maybe they just want to get rid of you. God is not moved by your emotions. God is also not moved by your shouting. Some of us like to shout, thinking that shouting will make God hear us better. God is not moved by all those things. Shouting is good; emotion is good; crying is good — they can be an indication of a heartfelt prayer or of a strong need. However, they must be based on *his* promises. Every answerable prayer must be based on God's precious promises. Therefore it is our responsibility to find out what he has promised and take it back to him in prayer. If God did not promise you something, your prayer, no matter how loud and intense, cannot force him to do it.

3. You must claim the promises for yourself.

After knowing the promises, you must then claim the promises for yourself. That is a very important step. It is not just enough to know God's promises; you must get to a point where you know that those promises are for you personally. Knowing the promises can make you feel good, but knowing them is not enough to make you experience them.

I must get to the point in my walk with God that when I am reading the Scriptures I am not just reading a history book—for a lot of us that is how we read the Scriptures. I must get to the point that when I am reading about Joseph or Abraham or someone else, I am not just reading about some people who lived several thousands of years ago. I must get to a point where I know that those stories have a bearing on my life through Christ and they are in fact personal letters from God to me. That is when you can gain the confidence required for the reward; that is when you can have the faith to hold on to the promises.

We had mentioned earlier how the children of Israel claimed God's promise and how that led to a great rescue from slavery in Egypt. However, when you read Exodus 12:40, you will notice that the Bible says the children of Israel actually spent four hundred *and thirty* years in Egyptian slavery. Why did they spend thirty years more than God intended? Was this an error? I don't think so. God said they were supposed to spend four hundred years but they spent four hundred and thirty years. Look what the Bible says:

Now the length of time the Israelite people lived in Egypt was 430 years.

—Exodus 12:40

This is also confirmed in the New Testament.

What I mean is this: The law, introduced 430 years later, does not set aside the covenant previously established by God and thus do away with the promise.

—Galatians 3:17

The Law was given in the same year that Israel left Egypt, also indicating that the children of Israel spent 430 years in Egypt. Why was this so? I have a feeling that this is because the Israelites did not start claiming the promise of God in time, and I will show you why.

There are two kinds of God's promises: unconditional and conditional. The unconditional promises of God are the kind of promises that do not require any action from us to come to pass. An example of such a promise is that Jesus will return the same way he was taken to heaven (see Acts 1:11). This promise will happen whether we pray about it or not. However, the majority of God's promises to us belong to the second category, the conditional promises of God. They require a corresponding action from us, and one of the required actions is claiming them. This implies that not claiming those promises can result in missing them, even though God intended them for us. This is a very important truth to note. Again, let's look at another scripture to prove this:

> Let us therefore fear, lest, a promise being left us of entering into his rest, any of you should seem to come short of it. For unto us was the gospel preached, as well as unto them: but the word preached did not profit them, not being mixed with faith in them that heard it.
>
> —Hebrews 4:1–2 KJV

What is this scripture warning us of? Even though we have the promise of entering into God's rest, we should be very careful not to miss out on it. To prove himself, the Holy Spirit through the writer said, "You know what? The original recipients of the promise actually missed out on the promise because they did not mix it with faith." One of the ways you mix the promise with faith is claiming the promise. We are generally admonished not to fear in the Bible, but in this case the Bible prompts us to fear missing God's promise. Missing God's promise is missing God's purpose and plan, and what is our life without his purpose.

4. You must exercise patience and persistence.

> We do not want you to become lazy, but to imitate those who through faith and patience inherit what has been promised.
>
> —Hebrews 6:12

There are certain people who inherit what God has promised; those who exercise faith and patience. Please permit me to repeat this again here: You can only inherit what God has promised. If God didn't promise it, you don't need to bother about it. If you are praying that your husband should die, or your wife should die because you don't like something about them, don't bother about that. God is not going to honor that prayer, because he didn't promise you that. A wife or husband may say, "Instead of me having to submit to this man or love this woman as Christ loves the Church, I'd rather pray that he or she dies," but you know that God did not promise that, and he is not going to honor such prayer. Some people even tout their prayer: "I am going to pray against you and you are going to see what is going to happen to you." That is as a result of ignorance. You only pray God's promises and not your fleshly feelings.

The Bible says we should not be lazy at claiming God's promise. Many of us are lazy at claiming God's promise. Don't be lazy. "Imitate those who through faith and patience inherit what has been promised." Many times we mistake *patience* as a passive word. *Patience* is not a passive word; it is an active word. When you are waiting on God you are doing something. You are claiming; you are praising him; you are thanking him; you are confessing those words. You are sleeping with it; you are waking with it. You are saying, "Thank you, Jesus, for what you are doing." You are waiting and you are working. That is why he says: "Don't be lazy." Life is not for lazy people; God's promises are not for lazy people.

I once heard a funny story about a man who won an award as the laziest man on earth. Yes, he won a *Guinness Book of World Records* award as the laziest man on earth. They wanted to give him his award and the gift, so they went to his house, and when they got there they were told by the neighbors, "He is not in the house. He is always at the beach just lying there and having fun; that is why he won the award." So they went to meet him at the beach. The guy was lying around and just enjoying the sun and the beach. They said, "Hey, man! Congratulations. You just won an award. You are the laziest man on earth. Here is the envelope with your check." The man replied,"Can you please roll me around and put the check in my pocket?" No wonder he won the laziest man award.

A lot of Christians are like that—we want God to roll us over and shuffle the promise into our pocket. That is not going to happen. Don't be lazy, but "imitate those who through faith and patience inherit what has been promised." That is how we obtain the promise.

5. In Christ Jesus God always says yes to his promises.

For no matter how many promises God has made, they are "Yes" in Christ. And so through him the "Amen" is spoken by us to the glory of God.

—2 Corinthians 1:20

Jesus Christ is the ultimate promise of God. Every promise made by God is fulfilled in Christ Jesus. In fact, Christ is the embodiment of everything God has planned for us through his promises. Without Christ, the promises of God are empty and without any real value. If you are reading this book and you have not accepted Jesus Christ as your personal Lord and Savior, it will be of no value. God only says yes to his promises in Christ Jesus. Sometimes people ask if this is also applicable to the promises in the Old Testament. The simple answer is yes. Look at what the Bible says below about the Law.

For Christ is the fulfillment of the law for righteousness to everyone who believes.

—Romans 10:4 WEB

The real purpose of the Law is to reveal Christ. The main point of all those seemingly confusing and convoluted rules, ordinances, regulations, and rituals is actually Christ. Every requirement of the Law has been fulfilled in Christ Jesus. How about the prophets? Look at what the Bible says about the prophets:

In the past God spoke to our ancestors through the prophets at many times and in various ways, but in these last days he has spoken to us by his Son, whom he appointed heir of all things, and through whom also he made the universe.

— Hebrews 1:1-2

This is simply saying that everything God said or intended for us through the prophets has been summed up for us in Christ Jesus his son. What a powerful statement! Under the New Testament dispensation, nothing is useful without Christ. Christ is the summation of everything God intended for us through his Word and his promises.

This truth reverberates throughout the Scriptures and cannot be overemphasized. Let us also look at what the Bible says concerning God's promise to our father Abraham:

Christ redeemed us from the curse of the law by becoming a curse for us, for it is written: "Cursed is everyone who is hung on a pole." He redeemed us in order that the blessing given to Abraham might come to the Gentiles through Christ Jesus, so that by faith we might receive the promise of the Spirit.

— Galatians 3:13–14

Look at what the Bible says here: Because of redemption, the blessing that was originally giving to Abraham becomes ours through Christ Jesus. Isn't that amazing? I would like to let you know that this fact is also true of other promises in the Bible. Jesus Christ is our connector and qualifier for all the promises of God. Jesus Christ is God's *yes* to his promises to us. When we accept him as our Lord and Savior, it is our *amen* to God's *yes*. It is only in him and through him that we can say "Amen" and hear "Yes" to God's promises. It may be true that your name was not specifically mentioned in the Bible, it is true that none of those sixty-six books were originally penned to you directly, but when you are in Christ Jesus, the promises are automatically transferred into your name. Jesus is the reason for everything God does. All things were made by him and for him (see Colossians 1:16), and he has been appointed heir of all things. When we accept him as our Lord and Savior, we become co-heir with him. That is why the Bible says in Romans 8:17, "Now if we are children, then we are heirs — heirs of God and co-heirs with Christ."

The other side of this truth is also very important. Without Jesus Christ all those stories, promises, prophecies, and prayers in the Bible are irrelevant and completely inapplicable to you. Christ is the reason why the great power that brought deliverance to the children of Israel from the bondage of the Egyptians can become ours. Outside of Christ I have no access to the great deliverance of Daniel from the lion's den. And the favor in the life of Joseph cannot be extended to me outside of Christ. Without Christ all those things you read in the Bible are just wonderful stories, good for the people you are reading about but of no bearing to you. Only Christ makes all those powerful stories and promises relevant and applicable.

Chapter 4

Positioned by Promises

We have learned about the power of God's promises. To get into God's plan and to be positioned by God through his GPS, you must know and claim the promises, learn to exercise patience, and understand that God's promises are applicable to you only in Christ Jesus. In this chapter we are going to examine some of these promises before we learn how to be positioned by them. This is very important because I want this fact to be as practical as possible; I want it to be something you can personally make use of. I want your life to be radically and fundamentally changed for good because of the truth presented by this book. My prayer for you is that after reading this book you will have a testimony to show that you have hooked up with God's plan for your life and you can live with confidence that you are in God's purpose.

Many of the scriptures I will share in this chapter I have personally used; in fact many of them I use on a weekly basis. I can personally refer to them as my life guard. I believe strongly that the greatest benefit of giving your life to Christ, apart from going to heaven, is your ability to know God's plan for your life, your ability to know God's mind, your ability to understand where God is leading you, your ability to figure out what God is doing in your life and what he wants you to do. This is my heart's desire for you: that through this book you will learn how to claim God's promises for you and also to live by them.

There is abundance of evidence in the Scriptures that shows that God doesn't want a single child of his to live in confusion. No matter how unrighteous you think you are, no matter how crooked you think you are as a believer, you are a child of God. As long as you have genuinely accepted Jesus as your personal Lord and Savior, he is going to clean you up. Whether you like it or not, God has a way of cleaning us up. I have learned that. Some people seem like they are not doing fine today, but in five years they may be the ones who are preaching to you. I have seen that over and over again. Some people might look like they are unserious today, when God is done with them, they will start giving testimony. The fact that you picked up this book to read or that you still make it to church once in a while tells me that God is doing something in your life, and that God is working in you. You are a work in progress, and he is not finished with you yet.

Let's look at the first promise. This is my favorite when it comes to knowing God's direction.

> I will instruct you and teach you in the way you should go; I will counsel you with my loving eye on you. Do not be like the horse or the mule, which have no under-standing but must be controlled by bit and bridle or they will not come to you.
>
> —Psalm 32:8-9

Unfortunately, many times we relate with God just like horses and mules. We live our lives just any way we please without paying attention to God's voice. It is only those times we are about fall into a ditch or hit the wall that God pulls the bit to prevent a disaster. While we don't get the full benefit of being led and guided by God, God doesn't allow us to crash or perish, because we are his children. We are not proactive in our wanting to hear him, but he steps in to prevent us from getting into serious trouble. When you live like that you are always going from crisis to crisis. You make bad choices, you fall into the ditch, you pray—or some believers pray—and God gets you out of it, and then you continue on and again make bad choices. If that describes your life, I want to let you know that it is not God's plan for you.

God says, "Come to me, I will instruct you in the way you should go." The purpose of this promise is for you to go to

God every day and say, "God, please instruct me. Teach me the way I should go. Counsel me and watch over me. I don't want to be like mules and donkeys that have no understanding. Give me understanding. I want to know your will. I want to know your plan for my life." That should be your prayer. If you pray this every day of your life, can you imagine how your life will turn out to be? Can you imagine if you had spent the last five, ten, or fifteen years claiming this promise? This is God's promise; he can never lie. He made the promise because he desires to lead you. You must respond by claiming the promise in prayer.

There is nothing for God in your failure. He is personally invested in your success. That is why he gave you that promise; he wants to lead you into a life of fulfillment and success. In fact, God wants to tell your success story; he wants to brag about you. In the book of Job we are told of how God brags about Job, how he says to the devil, "Have you seen Job, my servant?" (see Job 1:8) That is God; he is more interested in your success than you are. He wants to brag about you. He is interested in you. Go ahead and claim his promises.

Let's move to the next promise.

> Whether you turn to the right or to the left, your ears will hear a voice behind you, saying, "This is the way; walk in it."

> —Isaiah 30:21

I want you to think about the scripture above. Look at how specific it is. It clearly reveals God's intention for you. Again, yours is to grab that intention and say, "God, you promised to lead me. You promised I will hear your voice behind me. As I am going to work today, as I am going to that meeting today, let me hear your voice. I want to hear your voice concerning my career, my business, and my relationship." This is how to live by God's word. This is how to claim God's promise. Can you imagine the confidence you will have if you can hear his voice at every juncture of your life? Can you imagine the quality of the life you will live if at every moment of decision you can say, "I heard him saying go this way or that way"?

That is God's will for you, and anything less than that should be unacceptable. We can have that if we are willing to claim the promise in Christ Jesus.

Let's go to the next one.

> The Sovereign Lord has given me a well-instructed tongue, to know the word that sustains the weary. He wakens me morning by morning, wakens my ear to listen like one being instructed. The Sovereign Lord has opened my ears; I have not been rebellious, I have not turned away.
>
> —Isaiah 50:4–5

Yes, this is Prophet Isaiah talking here, giving a testimony of God's faithfulness in his life. He said, "God wakens my ear to listen." The truth is, that can be your testimony too, in Christ Jesus, if you can claim the promise. God is not a partial God: If he did it for Isaiah, he can do it for you. Do you want an instructed tongue? Do you want to be taught by God? Go ahead and claim the promise. Sometimes promises come by way of affirmations; this is one of those affirmations. Affirmations are to be confessed and proclaimed, they are revealing God's intention, and they are for us.

Let's go to the next one.

> For with you is the fountain of life; in your light we see light.
>
> —Psalm 36:9

I really love this verse: in his light we see light. Light represents clarity, direction, and understanding. Darkness represents confusion, chaos, and misunderstanding. Ephesians 5:8 says, "For you were once darkness, but now you are light in the Lord. Live as children of light." The Bible also says that Jesus is the light (see John 1:4); he is the light that swallows darkness. When you become a believer you automatically have direct access to the light. How do you use this scripture? It becomes your confession, and you to say, "Lord, I thank you because through you I am connected to the fountain of life, and in your light I see light." It is also one of those affirmation promises in the scripture.

Let's move to the next one, now in the New Testament.

My sheep listen to my voice; I know them, and they follow me.

—John 10:27

That is Jesus talking: People who belong to me follow me because they listen and know my voice. Are you his sheep? If you are a follower of the Lord Jesus, you must be a sheep. *People who are my sheep, they listen to my voice. They always wait until I speak and they follow. They don't just go ahead and do dumb things.* Every time we do dumb things, it is because we do not listen to him. I am sure you can testify that this is true in your life, that those times you didn't listen are the times you did dumb things. I'm sure you can say, "If I had listened, I wouldn't have done it." Jesus said, "My sheep listen to my voice; I know them, and they follow me." In John 10 Jesus describes the role of the shepherd. He said:

His sheep follow him because they know his voice. But they will never follow a stranger; in fact, they will run away from him because they do not recognize a stranger's voice.

—John 10:4–5

I love that scripture. I love to pray, "Lord, please train my ears; I want to be a sheep that doesn't recognize a stranger's voice." He also said they don't listen to strangers. Have you been listening to strange voices that are not of God? You need to claim this scripture for yourself. How do you use the scripture? You simply declare, "Lord Jesus, I am your sheep, therefore I listen to you; I refuse to listen to the voice of strangers. Train my ears to recognize your voice and to not recognize that of strangers."

If you have a son or daughter, you might be able to relate to this beter. Your children know your voice. In fact, they know the voice of your car; they know how it sounds. They know when your car pulls into the driveway. That is how much God wants us to know his voice. He wants us to be able to say, "That is God talking; God is saying something. I don't have the clearance; my heart doesn't flow in that direction." God wants us as believers to care greatly about what he thinks about our situation. If you are truly his sheep you will wait until you hear what he says about your situation before you act.

> But when he, the Spirit of truth, comes, he will guide you into all the truth. He will not speak on his own; he will speak only what he hears, and he will tell you what is yet to come.
>
> —John 16:13

The Bible says whosoever is born of God has the Holy Spirit in him (see Romans 8:9). If you are a child of God, you have the Spirit of God inside of you. The Bible says the job of the Holy Spirit is to guide you. You are not meant to be without a guardian. I want you to say, "Holy Spirit, please guide me."

Look at another scripture:

> The Spirit himself testifies with our spirit that we are God's children.
>
> —Romans 8:16

If you are God's child, the Holy Spirit testifies with your spirit. The Holy Spirit communicates with your spirit. God did not give you the Holy Spirit without a purpose. The Holy Spirit is in you to communicate the will of God with your spirit. Your role is to listen to the Holy Spirit, to engage your spirit with the Holy Spirit, to stop listening to strangers, and to listen to what he is telling you.

> Do not conform to the pattern of this world, but be transformed by the renewing of your mind. Then you will be able to test and approve what God's will is—his good, pleasing and perfect will.
>
> —Romans 12:2

That is what we should be doing as believers, testing and approving what God's will is, not just living life the way it comes. When you get a job offer, you ask God, "God, is that what you want me to do?" You may say, "Well, I don't know about this hearing God thing, it is very difficult and confusing." Yes, it is for those who refuse to claim the promises. Start by claiming the promises first, and then watch the fulfillment to those promises as he begins to show you his will. God knows how he does his things; he knows how to bring you to that place where you begin to know his will. Yours is to apply your faith and begin to say, "God, I won't do anything unless you ask me to; Lord, what are you saying concerning this situation?"

Maybe you are afraid of making mistakes and you are saying, "What if I assume this is God speaking to me and it turns out not to be so?" Don't let fear of failure stop you. God knows our frailty, he know you are going to make mistakes once in a while. The most important thing for you is the desire to know his will. God is not supprised or disappointed by your mistakes, he knows they are as a result of our limitation and not a deliberate disobedience or a lifestyle choice. The fact is that your mistakes can't stop God's plan for your life, he has already factored your mistakes into things. That is why the bible says "in all things God works for the good of those who love him, who have been called according to his purpose." (Romans 8:28).

Let's go to the next promise.

For this reason, since the day we heard about you, we have not stopped praying for you. We continually ask God to fill you with the knowledge of his will through all the wisdom and understanding that the Spirit gives.

—Colossians 1:9

This is a prayer of Apostle Paul for the Colossian church, and it is one of the Holy Spirit–inspired prayers in the Bible. Implied in this prayer is the promise of God to fill us with the knowledge of his will. Remember, all God's promises are yours in Christ. This prayer is not just for the Colossian church, it is also for you and me through Christ. You can also pray and say, "Lord, fill me with the knowledge of your will; give me so much spiritual wisdom and understanding that when I look at any situation, I know what is your will. When I get into any situation, I just know this is what you want me to do." Let that be your daily prayer and watch what God will do.

Let's go to the last one.

> For God hath not given us a spirit of fear; but of power, and of love, and of a sound mind.
>
> —2 Timothy 1:7 KJV

A sound mind is a mind that is complete, clear, not confused, not perplexed, not mesmerized, and not shaky. It is a mind that can discern God's will easily. It is what the Bible refers to as the mind of Christ (1 Corinthians 2:16). It is God's will that we operate in the mind of Christ, that way we are able to make accurate and godly decisions. This scripture clearly states God's will for us to appropriate through prayer and confession.

God wants us to live in reckless abandonment to his will. He wants us to come to him and say, "God, what is your will for me?" I was recently sharing with a single brother and I said, "It is not popular anymore when you say, 'Go to God and pray about whom you are going to marry.'" People don't fast about things like that anymore. In fact, if you talk like that today, people start laughing at you. That is one of the reasons there are so many marriages in trouble today in the Church of God — we have stopped listening to him.

I am not saying you should simply pray and ignore your responsibility in finding someone to marry, or that you should use your spirituality to manipulate the other person. Obviously some people are taking the idea of hearing God in this area to the extreme. A brother can't just go to a sister and say, "God said I should marry you. I saw you in a dream and the angel said you are my wife." That is a bastardization of the concept, but it does not alter the fact that you should seek God's direction concerning who you should marry. You should know; you should be sure this is who God is leading you to marry.

If you are not hearing God, if you are still living in darkness, confused, unsure, and without confidence, it is not because God does not want to lead you, it is simply because you are not learning how to hear him. I want to remind you again: Every blessing from God starts with a promise, and it is your responsibility to find out his promises and claim them for yourself. We have looked at a number of those promises. Start by claiming them daily and watch yourself grow in his knowledge.

Chapter 5

Pre-decision

Therefore, when Christ came into the world, he said: "Sacrifice and offering you did not desire, but a body you prepared for me; with burnt offerings and sin offerings you were not pleased. Then I said, 'Here I am—it is written about me in the scroll—I have come to do your will, my God.'"

—Hebrews 10:5-7

GPS is a powerful tool, but as powerful as the GPS is, there is a category of people that the GPS system cannot help. Those are people who cannot admit ignorance or listen to simple instruction. In order to be helped by the GPS, you've got to trust the GPS enough to follow the directions given to you.

For some people, it takes time to trust any technology. I migrated to the United States from Nigeria in 1998, and I remember in my early months in the U.S. it was hard for me to trust the ATM machine. Actually, I would say withdrawing money was a lot easier, but making deposits into the machine was very difficult for me. For months I wouldn't put my money in the machine. I would say to myself, "What if the machine doesn't know or forgets that I put in my money, or what if the machine mistakes my money with someone else's?" The first few instances that I put money in the ATM, I would go back home and call the bank, or go on the Internet and checked to confirm that my money was actually deposited into my account. After a while the ATM earned my trust, and I hardly go inside the bank anymore. In fact, nowadays I only go inside the bank if the ATM cannot perform my transaction. Even now I know some people still find it very hard to use the ATM. I met someone who told me he would rather go to the person inside the bank. He said, "That is the only way I know that my money actually gets in my account."

Some people find it hard to trust any technology. Even when the GPS is telling them to go to the left, they say, "I am not sure what this machine is talking about." They still get out their map and try to confirm the GPS directions. Some would try to rationalize the directions based on their prior understanding. Others will get additional directions from somewhere else as a backup plan and compare it with those from the GPS as they travel along. These kinds of people don't get much help from the GPS. They usually end up getting confused and lost.

The same principle is applicable to submitting to God's GPS. It requires a great deal of trust. First we must know and be fully convinced that God has a good plan for us. When we understand that God integrates every circumstance in our life to accomplish his will for us, it is easier to trust him. Even those times when we don't understand what he is saying or when we can't figure it out or even when he seems wrong based on our own understanding—there are times God's wisdom will seem like foolishness in our eyes—we are still able to trust him when we are convinced of his love for us.

I want to start by showing you a very good and important verse of the Scripture. This scripture provides crucial support for what I am talking about in this chapter.

> By myself I can do nothing; I judge only as I hear, and my judgment is just, for I seek not to please myself but him who sent me.
>
> —John 5:30

If you are wondering who made this statement, it is Jesus Christ himself. Here he gives us the secret, a very important secret of how he makes decisions. He said, "By myself I can do nothing; I judge only as I hear." For you not to be confused, the word *judge* here is actually from the Greek word *krino. Krino* means to pick out, to select, to choose. It means to resolve. It is a very broad word, but it generally implies a process of selecting among many options. So Jesus is saying, "I judge [I make decisions, I pick out, I consider, I choose, and I compare and make determinations] only as I hear, and my judgment [or my decision] is just [or right or righteous]." In other words, Jesus is saying here, "I make righteous or correct decisions." Why do I make correct decisions? "For [or because] I seek not to please myself but him who sent me." Because I have made a pre-decision to do whatever he tells me to do, before he ever tells me, I can hear him correctly.

If Jesus is telling us the secret of his success in hearing God, he is also giving us a major reason why many of us can't hear God. It is because we have not made that pre-decision. If you are the type of person that when God calls you and say, "I want to tell you to do something, are you going to do it?" and you say, "Let me hear it first," then you cannot hear God. God doesn't want us to deal with him like that. You can't say, "Just tell me first, and then I will know." God wants us to make a decision that whatever he tells us to do we will do, even before we know what he is going to say. That is the secret of Jesus. He said, "I do nothing by myself. I only make the decisions that I hear from him, and the reason why I make good decisions is because I don't plan to please myself. My goal is to please him who sent me."

I would like to show you another scripture that complements what we have just talked about.

> I will instruct you and teach you in the way you should go; I will counsel you with my loving eye on you. Do not be like the horse or the mule, which have no understanding but must be controlled by bit and bridle or they will not come to you.
>
> —Psalm 32:8–9

The first part of verse 9 is very important. God says, "Do not be like the horse or the mule." That is the New International Version Bible translation. I would like to show you some other translations of the same scripture.

54

Do not be like a senseless horse or mule that needs a bit and bridle to keep it under control.

—Psalm 32:9 NLT

Don't be stupid like horses and mules that must be led with ropes to make them obey.

—Psalm 32:9 CEV

Sometimes God has to lead us with ropes. Some of those times it is just to save us and to make sure we do not veer off into the ditch. Other times he has to lead us by taking us through a painful process. If you are wondering what a bridle and a bit are, they are equipment used to control a horse. A bit is a bar that goes into the mouth of a horse and rests on its mouth. It is what the horse is biting on. A bridle is the whole system, and includes both the headstall that holds the bit and the reins that are attached to the bit. This system is what is used to control a horse by exerting pressure on sensitive areas of its face. Why is this needed? It is because horses simply don't listen, and the person who rides the horse has to jerk and pull the bridle. It is not a very convenient thing for the horse, and it is very painful for the horse. It is because of the pain that the horse will listen and follow the direction of the rider.

Let us now try to understand what God is saying here. He is saying, "I don't want you to be like horses or mules that have to be taken through a painful process before they can listen or take instruction." Sometimes God has to do something like that for some of us. He literally has to make sure you crash; he has to make sure you hit the road somewhere. He has to make sure you suffer some pain before you realize what he is saying to you. So he is telling us here, "This is not good for you. I don't want to treat you like that. I want you to be so sensitive that you can understand my winking or simply my looks."

If you have children I am sure you perfectly understand what I am talking about. Your child is behaving badly, doing something stupid and embarrassing in public, and you are winking at him and he is not listening. With your wink you are saying to him or her, "Look, I don't want you to do something stupid," or "I want you to stop behaving badly in public." It is usually a situation you as a parent are not happy about, and you want your child to be quick to listen or sensitive to your correction. That is what God is saying: "I am instructing you gently; I am winking at you. I don't want you to be like mules and donkeys."

The summary of the message here is this: Our ability to hear God depends on our willingness to obey him. Unless you have made a pre-decision to obey him without condition, God will not waste his time speaking to you. God is not talkative; he speaks only to people who listen. He speaks only to people who have decided to listen and obey even before he speaks. Pre-decision is the secret of Jesus and also the key to our success in hearing God.

Chapter 6

Surrender

Whoever wants to be my disciple must deny themselves and take up their cross and follow me. For whoever wants to save their life will lose it, but whoever loses their life for me will find it.

— Matthew 16:24–25

The word *surrender* is very easy to understand. To surrender means to give up control, to yield authority or power to someone else. That is why when the police come to arrest people and they ask them to surrender, people raise their two hands. The raising of two hands is a sign of surrender. You give total authority and control of yourself to the other person, usually a person who is of higher authority. Another scriptural word that conveys this same meaning is *consecration*. Consecration simply means to offer yourself or make a solemn dedication of yourself to a special purpose or service. There is probably no other portion of the Scripture that describes consecration better than a passage in the Apostle Paul's letter to the Roman church. Let us take a look at the passage:

> Therefore, I urge you, brothers and sisters, in view of God's mercy, to offer your bodies as a living sacrifice, holy and pleasing to God — this is your true and proper worship. Do not conform to the pattern of this world, but be transformed by the renewing of your mind. Then you will be able to test and approve

what God's will is—his good, pleasing and perfect will.

—Romans 12:1–2

Ultimately this is what God is saying: "I want you to be able to know my will. I want you to be able to test and approve what my will is, but you will have to do a few things to get there." A few things have to happen in your life before you get to that point. In the GPS world, the GPS receiver is generally open to many other signals. There are many signals out there, each of them at different frequencies and wavelengths. Your device is made in such a way that it knows what signals to accept and process. That is what the Bible is saying in the scripture above. You need to be able to test and approve the signals. It is not every voice speaking to you that is of God; there are many others voices fighting for your attention. You need to be able to differentiate between those voices and determine which is of God and which is not.

In John 10:4–5, which we read earlier, Jesus said, "My sheep hear my voice and the voice of a stranger they will not hear. They hear my voice because they recognize my voice." As the shepherd is speaking, there are strangers also speaking. Isn't that always the case? You are always hearing different voices, but he says, "If you do offer yourself as a living sacrifice, you will be able to test and approve what God's will for you is."

The Bible says in Isaiah 30:21: "Whether you turn to the right or to the left, your ears will hear a voice behind you, saying, 'This is the way; walk in it." *The* problem is that sometimes the voice is telling you to go to the left, and another voice is telling you to go to the right. God is telling you to go forward, and something or someone else is telling you to turn back. Isn't that one of our problems? Competing voices on one issue or many different options about a particular matter—how do you know when God is the one speaking? The key here is surrender.

There are three things mentioned here that are critical to living a surrendered life, and we are going to examine each of them. I would like you to please pay attention and take these scriptures seriously. It is very important to meditate on them carefully as you read.

1. Sacrificial living

The first thing the scripture says is "Offer your bodies as living sacrifices, holy and pleasing to God." This is talking about sacrificial living. That is the first condition.

Apostle Paul was saying this to people who understood what sacrifice is. It is harder for most of us in the Western world, especially in this day and age, to really understand what sacrifice means. Unfortunately, without an understanding of the word *sacrifice*, we may not be able to grasp what Apostle Paul is talking about as easily as the original recipients of the letter would have. He was writing to the church in Rome, the majority of whom were Jewish, and if there is anything about the Jewish people at the time, they understood what sacrifice is. They spent every day of their lives sacrificing one thing or the other to God. There were some mandated sacrifices for different things. Every time they were going through something, when they gave birth to a child, if they were looking up to God for something, or if they had done something wrong, they offered a sacrifice to God. Every major event in their lives was marked by a sacrifice. In some seasons of the year they had to offer certain sacrifices to God. These were stipulated in the Law of Moses and it was their way of life.

This is how a sacrifice works: You take your sacrifice, which is usually an animal such as a goat, a lamb, or a turtledove, and you take it to the altar and offer it to God. You go meet a priest and tell the priest, "I want to offer this kind of sacrifice." The priests would take the animal that you brought, kill it, drain the blood, and put the animal on the altar. They would then set it on fire and burn it. Sometimes they would use the ashes for the ritual. Sometimes the priests or you would eat parts of the animal and throw other parts away. Other times they would cut parts of the animal and give it to you to take back home, depending on the prescription according to the Law of Moses. When it came to sacrifices, the Jewish people had a lot of experience, so when Apostle Paul used the word *sacrifice,* he was really speaking their language.

There is one thing about sacrifice: By the time you are performing all those rituals, the animal is already dead, and so the animal does not protest. It is a very easy process. When Paul says here, "Offer your bodies as living sacrifices," not a dead one, he was making a significant distinction. I would imagine that a living sacrifice would be a little challenging, because you are offering an animal that is alive, that can protect itself and run away. When you offer yourself to God as a living sacrifice, you still have the opportunity to protest, ask questions, or simply run away. As a living sacrifice, you are wondering, "What is the priest doing with me?" That is a significant difference between a living and a dead sacrifice. A living sacrifice wants to know what the priest is doing. That is always the issue. That is why it must be an active, deliberate, and continuous process. It is a daily offering of your body. It is a daily surrendering of yourself, of your physical body, of your entire existence. Jesus wants everything about your life: your desire, your disappointment, your joy, your aspiration, your position, your possessions, your will, your present, and your future. He wants everything: all you are, all you will be, and all you want. He wants it laid down at the altar and sur-rendered to him. What a challenging step!

Partial surrendering ensures you never know the will of God for your life. Total surrender puts you in the path of knowing God's plan and purpose for you. Total surrender means every possession you have is no longer yours. Paul puts it this way in another passage of the Scripture, while describing his own life. He says, "It is no longer I who live, but Christ lives in me" (Galatians 2:20 NLT). Every effort of your life should be centered on Christ. When you hold something back from him, you are literally saying to him, "You are not worthy of it."

"Offer your bodies as living sacrifices, holy and pleasing to God—this is your spiritual act of worship." That is what worship is. It is your spiritual act of worship. Worship is more than just singing and raising your hands. He is saying that your spiritual act of worship is your decision to offer God your life and everything associated with it: your dreams, your goals, your ambition, your possessions, your position, and your vision.

How do you do that? It starts by going to him and telling him sincerely—and it has to be a daily telling, not just a one-time event—"Lord, I offer my life to you; I offer everything to you. All that I am, all that I will ever be, all that I have, all that I will ever have, I declare them as yours." You say to him, "Whatever you tell me to do I will do; wherever you tell me to go I will go." Those are daily offerings of your body. "Offer your bodies as living sacrifices, holy and pleasing to God—this is your spiritual act of worship."

That is what God wants, that is how you worship him, which is your spiritual act of worship. That is what makes whatever you do meaningful. All those things we associate with worship—singing, dancing, kneeling down, crying, praying, etc.—are only meaningful after we have performed the real spiritual act of worship. Without the spiritual act of worship, all those physical and emotional actions will be just meaningless religious activities.

The reason is that anybody can do all those things; anybody can sing, "I surrender all to Jesus," when they don't really mean to surrender anything to him. Jesus said, "These people honor me with their lips, but their hearts are far from me" (Matthew 15:8). Can you imagine that? How did Jesus know that? It's because he can see the heart. Jesus is talking to the Pharisees here. They are very good at worshipping; they are very good at singing; they are very good at jumping, praying, fasting, and all that religious stuff, but he said, "Whenever I ask them to do something, they don't do it. Some of them even spiritualize it. Some of them even quote the Scripture to say why they can't do what I ask them to do." However they have mastered the acts associated with worship, they know the right phrases to use, the right tone, diction, and the expressions to make worship look awesome, but their hearts are not engaged in it.

I want to challenge you to offer yourself to him today. When you truly offer yourself to him, you escape a life of confusion. The reason why we live in darkness and confusion, not knowing what the will of God is, is because we have not offered ourselves to him as a living sacrifice. Sometimes we offer him some aspects of our lives that we are comfortable with. We say to him, "I can offer you this part, but this area I don't want to offer." Some aspects of our lives are very easy to offer to God. Some people offer their time but not their money. Some people find it easier to offer their money than their pride or ambition. Jesus wants it all. He is either Lord of all or no Lord at all. Partial surrender is no surrender at all.

I remember when I was still in college, and I went to one of those seminars about relationships. The speaker, a Christian relationship expert, spent a good deal of time teaching us about how to find and know the person you are to marry. I was a very young believer then, and this speaker kept talking about what all we would be "receiving from God." Do this and "you are going to receive from God,"; "when you pray and receive instruction from God . . ." "Receiving from God" was a very popular phrase among Christian students during my years in college. It simply meant God speaking to you about whom to marry. The whole idea of receiving from God about whom to marry was very strange, confusing, and scary to me at the time. I didn't understand it at all. After the seminar I was returning back to the hostel with another brother who was a more matured Christian, and we were talking about the lessons from the seminar. I said to him, "I don't understand this whole idea of receiving from God about whom to marry. My fear is this: What if I decide to receive from God and God gives me a handicapped person?" The brother replied, "Whatever God offers you, be sure that you are going to like it." I thought that was a very good answer. Many of us have this same problem about surrendering to God: We are afraid God is going to give us something we don't like. But the fact is that God knows what is good for us better than we do, and we just have to learn to trust him.

It is a wrong approach to say to God, "I give you this part of my life but I'm not sure the other part." We must all come to that point in our life where we lay everything on the altar as a sacrifice. If you have not gotten to that point in your Christian life, it is impossible to hear from him and locate his plan and purpose for your life. It is called a life of consecration, and you can never enjoy your walk with God until you get to that point. Without consecration your walk with God is going to be full of crises. God has to be using bit and bridle to pull you here and there every once in a while because you are about to get into some dangerous ground. God sometimes has to allow you to just hit the wall. God has to go block you sometimes, get you into crisis so you can know his will because he loves you. But that is not how you want to live. You don't want to live your life moving from one crisis to another. The only way to true happiness is by trusting and obeying God.

When you get to a point of absolute consecration, serving God becomes a beautiful experience, a sweet experience like that told by the Psalmist: "Taste and see that the Lord is good; blessed is the one who takes refuge in him" (Psalm 34:8). That should be your goal. I want to encourage you to get into a life of true surrender. It is a life without any other agenda than to please God. Jesus said, "My judgment is just because I have no other agenda but to do what he tells me to do." I want you also to tell him, "God, I consecrate myself. I surrender myself. I refuse to harbor any other agenda apart from pleasing you. Whatever you tell me to do I will do. Wherever you tell me to go I will go. Whatever you tell me to say I will say." That is the mark of a life surrendered to God.

2. Separated living

The second thing Apostle Paul mentions is the idea of separated living. This is in verse 2 of the passage: "Do not conform any longer to the pattern of this world." This was a very real problem in those days, but it is an even bigger problem now. It means don't allow the world system to shape the way you think. The goal of the worldly system is to shape you, to shape your values, your priorities, your desires, and your motivation. It is softly happening to the body of Christ, but the Bible says, "Do not be conformed."

This is something we are confronting as a generation of believers. The worldly system is gradually shaping us. It is shaping our values, taste, thoughts, and language. If you study the book of Daniel chapter 1 very well, one of the things the king told them to do to Daniel and his peers is to change their language, their values and their thinking. But the Bible says, "Daniel resolved not to defile himself with the royal food and wine, and he asked the chief official for permission not to defile himself this way" (Daniel 1:8). That is what our worldly system wants to do to us. If you turn on the TV, listen to popular shows, watch talk shows or any Hollywood movie, or read the news, what they are attempting to do is to change your mindset and values. Unfortunately they have won many hearts, even the hearts of many believers. A lot of them might be doing some great things, such as feeding the poor, building schools in Africa, and helping people, but at the same time promoting an anti-Christian message and lowering the bar of morality by the way they live. They are gradually changing our values, even those of believers.

He said, "Do not be conformed to the pattern of this world." Jesus wants to shape us into his likeness. That is his goal, he wants us to be changed and transformed into his likeness, but we are confronting a culture that is competing with his plan for us. We must reject that culture. Paul is saying here, "Do not be conformed. Make up your mind not to follow the pattern of the world." For example, it is commonplace now for couples to live together before they get married. The arrangement is called cohabitation. There is a study out there that says more than two-thirds of married couples in the US say that they lived together before getting married. The sad part however is that gradually, even in church, cohabitation is becoming an accepted practice. People don't shiver or feel any kind of outrage over that anymore. Some say, "Oh, no big deal, they are going to marry each other anyway." We have lowered the standard of righteousness. Sex before marriage is no longer a taboo; this is because the church is gradually conforming to the pattern of the world.

Some time ago I was at a park in midtown New York City. I was working in that area at the time and it was during my lunch break. One of the things you find about midtown New York is that it is filled with homosexual practice. It is very common to see a man and man or woman and woman expressing love to each other openly. This particular day I was walking around in the park and I saw a young boy and girl kissing and caressing each other. They must have been in their early teens. Because I have seen so much worse, I thought to myself, "Thank God that at least it is a male and a female." But as soon as that thought came to me, I caught myself and corrected my thought: I said to myself, "It is not something to rejoice over just because I have seen worse things." Those were teenagers kissing and rolling on the ground in a public place, and everybody was just walking around, minding their own business. But that is how the world system works; we have been exposed and bombarded with so much immorality that anything less immoral gradually becomes righteousness to us. The standard has been so much lowered that even in our mind we are accepting things that ordinarily we would not have accepted based on God's Word. That is why the Bible says, "Do not conform."

I know the example I have just given is probably more distant for many of us; I want to encourage you to take it to a more personal level and apply it to your personal life. It is easy to look at issues happening out there. A lot of times those people don't even know God; hence in a sense they can do whatever they like. In your own life, where are you conforming? Are you conforming in your relationships, in your friendships? Are you practicing relative Christianity? Are you measuring yourself based on others whom you perceive are less righteous than you? That is not God's wisdom. The Bible says, "When they measure themselves by themselves and compare themselves with themselves, they are not wise" (2 Corinthians 10:12). That is how the world system works to get us to conform, but the Bible says, "Do not conform to the pattern of this world."

3. Sanctified thinking

The last thing Apostle Paul mentions is called sanctified thinking. Verse 2 also says, "But be transformed by the
renewing of your mind."

We have talked about sacrificial living, which is to offer
God everything you have, including your life. We have also
talked about separated living, which means refusing to be
conformed to the pattern of the world. The third thing we are
going to talk about is sanctified thinking.

God's Word Translation puts the phrase "renewing your
mind" as "change the way you think." The way you think
can only be changed by the Word of God. That is one of the
primary purposes of reading and meditating on the Word
of God. When you saturate yourself with the Word of God,
when you take in the Word of God regularly, when you look
for every opportunity to consume the Word of God and the
Word dwells richly in you, you will suddenly realize that your
thinking begins to change. The way you look at the world, the
way you look at things, the way you interpret what is going
on around you begin to change. You realize you are not necessarily excited by what many others around you are getting
excited about. You realize that you are no longer moved by
what other people around you are easily moved by. The way
you think begins to change.

When you immerse yourself in the Word of God, you also
realize that your desires begin to change. What is important to
you, your goals and your ambition, what you love and what
you hate begins to change. You begin see a gradual and at
some point sudden change in your attitude to life, to people,
and to things. That is what renewing of your mind means. Your
mind begins to function the way God originally designed it
to. Your mind is retrained to submit to your spirit. Your mind
no longer argues with the voice of your spirit. Only a renewed
mind can discern and accept the will of God. We have talked
about the soul as the place where our sinful tendency resides.
It is the seat of rebellion toward God. Even if your spirit has
been made alive in Christ Jesus and is receiving instructions

from the Holy Spirit, a mind not renewed will constantly reject the message of the spirit. That is why Apostle Peter says, "For you are receiving the end result of your faith, the salvation of your souls" (1 Peter 1:9). Apostle Peter was talking to believers here, so he wasn't talking about salvation as in regeneration; they were already saved. The salvation of your soul here is the renewal of your mind.

Without a surrendered life, locating and entering into God's plan and purpose for your life is impossible. Critical to a surrendered life is sacrificial living, separated living, and sanctified thinking. Apostle Paul concluded that when you do all these three things, then "you will be able to test and approve what God's will is" — then you will become a good receiver. You will no longer be described as saved but lost. You are in a position to effectively discern and locate God's plan for your life. What a beautiful life that will be.

What I later found out is that even among the GPS receivers, there are good ones and not so good ones. As the saying goes, you get what you pay for. If you go buy a very cheap brand, it may take forever to get the signal when you turn it on or to recalculate when you get lost. The problem is not the signal. The satellites are the same; the same signal is being sent to every GPS receiver. The problem is with the receiver. The quality of the receiver is first of all based on how quickly it recieves the signal. Some GPS receivers can even cause you to miss the road because it takes a long for them to calculate the direction for you. They are cheap and slow.

What the Bible is saying above is: If you live a sacrificial life, a separated life, and you have sanctified thinking, you become a good receiver. A good receiver knows how to process information received very well; it knows how to separate those signals that are bad from the good ones. Some of the GPS units these days even tell you when the traffic is heavy. I recently got a handheld GPS device that does that. I'll be driving along and it just tells me, "There is traffic ahead, do you want to reroute?" You click "yes" and it reroutes you. There is another feature in my GPS that I love, and it took me a while to figure it out. Sometimes when driving and I would hear, "Caution, caution, caution." I finally found out that this happens any time I go beyond the speed limit of the road I am traveling on, and it is cautioning me. It automatically knows the speed limit of the road and warns when you are driving above it. God wants to make you a good receiver. He wants you to get good signals. God wants to lead every one of us; in fact, he is sending a signal already. The issue is, are you a good receiver? Are you receiving the signal or are you mixing up God's signal with other signals?

Before you continue to read, I want you to take some time to pray at this juncture. I want you to say, "Lord, I want to be a good receiver. I want to engage in sacrificial living. I present my body a living sacrifice. I will no longer conform to the patterns of this world. I will be transformed by the renewing of my mind. Then I will be able to test and approve what your will is, your good, pleasing, and perfect will."

God is bringing this word to you for a purpose, for a reason. It is very crucial. I believe God is taking you to a different level in your relationship with him. God wants to take you from being just a baby to being a mature man or woman in the things of the Spirit. God wants to take you and change you from someone who just mumbles and fumbles through life. He wants to make you into someone who knows his ways, who understands his purpose, and who is positioned in his will.

I want you to take this moment and ask him, "Lord, I want to walk in your ways. I consecrate myself. I dedicate myself. I surrender my whole life. Take over. Take charge. I do not want to live any longer, but I want Christ to live through me."

Chapter 7

Background Noise

He says, "Be still, and know that I am God; I will be exalted among the nations, I will be exalted in the earth."

—Psalm 46:10

I firmly believe that God wants every one of his children to know what he has in his mind for them. It is not his plan that we live our lives confused; it is not his plan that we live our lives without knowing our purpose. It is also not his plan that we live our lives based on assumptions. If you are his child, more than anything else he wants to lead you; he wants to instruct you. The Bible says that with God there is no variableness; there is no shadow of turning (see James 1:17 NKJV). That means he doesn't lead some people and leave some people in confusion. That is not his nature; God does not show favoritism.

If you have two children, you don't say, "I am going to love this child because he is very good and because he is very smart, and I am not going to love this other child because he is not that smart." When people do that, we call it bad parenting. It always amazes me when I watch TV and I see someone has done something stupid, maybe they have just committed a crime and everyone is angry and talking about how bad and evil this person is, and all of a sudden the media will interview the parents and they will start by saying, "He is a good child, he is a loving child, we just don't know what happened." It's always amazing; sometimes I say to myself,

"Can't these people tell the truth?" But the truth is that parents love their children unconditionally. I want to announce to you that God loves you unconditionally. Don't say, "Maybe if I am a better Christian or if I can do this and that, God will love me more." The Bible says his love is everlasting; he loves you unconditionally.

I don't know what you are going through. I believe strongly that God has brought you in contact with this book for a reason. If you are confused and you are wondering, "What is my purpose in life? Where is God leading me to? How do I hear his voice and how do I know when he is speaking to me?" the Lord has brought you in contact with this book to encourage you and to let you know that he is interested in showing you where to go.

At this point I would like to do a recap of some of the critical things we have talked about. In two of the earlier chapters we examined God's promises. If knowing God's will is important to you, you start by claiming those promises, and the promises are abundant. The first step for you to take as a believer is to begin to find out his promises and begin to claim them for your life. That is how to get anything from God.

We have also examined, in the previous chapter titled "Surrender," some of the basic requirements to be led by God using the analogy of the GPS. There are certain people that the GPS cannot help. Those are the people who would not listen to the GPS; those are the people who do not trust the GPS. Some people don't trust any technology. I gave you an example of how I didn't trust ATM machines when I first moved into the United States. I would not put my money in that machine; I would rather go into the bank. Some of us have those trust issues with God, and we have to deal with that.

We should trust him, and our trust should lead into a life of reckless abandonment, where we trust his plan and trust his purpose for our life. It has to be a daily thing; it has to be something you do daily. You go before God and present yourself as a living sacrifice, lay yourself on the altar, and say, "Lord, please work in me. I am ready to do whatever you tell me to do." The condition is that you have to be willing to do what he wants you to do even before you know what he wants you to do.

We also examined the life of Jesus and we looked at an example of his statement in John 5:30, where he said, "By myself I can do nothing; I judge [make decisions] only as I hear, and my judgment [my decision] is just [right], for I seek not to please myself but him who sent me." If our goal is to do his will, whatever he tells us to do, we will know his will.

In this chapter, we are going to examine another fundamental key point that helps us to understand or to hear what God is saying. It is called background noise.

One of the things I notice in my car that came loaded with GPS is that when the GPS is speaking, all other noise (radio, DVD, etc.) will be automatically muted. That is one big difference between my car that comes loaded with the GPS and the other car that doesn't. The car that comes with GPS is programmed so that, whether you are listening to the radio, playing a DVD for the children in the back, or listening to music, every other noise stops once the GPS begins to give directions. Rightly the manufacturer knows that until all other noises stop you cannot clearly hear the voice of your GPS. In my other car, the handheld GPS is an external device and it is not linked to the other systems. Hence I have to find my own way of dealing with the issue of noise. In cases like that, when you have the GPS on, you have to manually lower the radio or any other device playing. The fact is, somehow you still have to be able to kill the background noise around you in order to hear clearly what the GPS is saying.

The same principle is very applicable in the things of the spirit. The reason why it is very applicable is because God speaks gently and softly. Even though he enjoys speaking to his children and he does, he speaks softly and gently. One of the attributes of God is that he is not feisty or argumentative. He is the almighty and all-powerful God; hence he doesn't need to be feisty. Only powerless people are feisty. God is all powerful, so when he speaks, he does so softly. He said in the book of Genesis, "My Spirit will not contend with humans forever, for they are mortal" (Genesis 6:3). In 1 Kings 19:11–13, when the prophet Elijah was trying to hear God, he thought he was going to hear the voice of God in a strong wind, an earthquake, or a fire, but the Bible says the Lord was not in any of those things. Eventually, the Bible says, "after the fire a still small voice" and Elijah "wrapped his face in his mantle and went out and stood in the entrance in of the cave" (NKJV). What a great lesson! When God speaks, he speaks in a still, small voice.

Hence, because of the way he speaks, to hear him we have to make sure we kill all the background noises that can prevent us from hearing. Jesus said in John 10, "My sheep hear my voice; the voice of a stranger they will not hear." One of our main problems is that there are always strangers speaking to us, and oftentimes those strange voices tend to be much louder, which prevents us from hearing the voice of God.

King Solomon, the wisest man that ever lived, wrote, "My son, if sinful men entice you, do not give in to them." (Proverbs 1:10) There are always enticements around us. Unfortunately it doesn't take much to get distracted. Have you ever found yourself speaking to someone and all of a sudden they get distracted and start listening to something else? Oftentimes it is because of some other noise around, such as TV, radio, music, or other kinds of noises. I have experienced this many times, and sometimes I would have to tell the person, "Can you please focus?" Other options are to kill the noise if possible or take the person out of the noisy area.

I would like us to read from 1 Kings 19. This is God speaking to Elijah.

> The Lord said, "Go out and stand on the mountain in the presence of the Lord, for the Lord is about to pass by."

> Then a great and powerful wind tore the mountains apart and shattered the rocks before the Lord, but the Lord was not in the wind. After the wind there was an earthquake, but the Lord was not in the earthquake. After the earthquake came a fire, but the Lord was not in the fire. And after the fire came a gentle whisper. When Elijah heard it, he pulled his cloak over his face and went out and stood at the mouth of the cave.

Then a voice said to him, "What are you doing here, Elijah?"

$-$1 Kings 19:11–13

Again, God speaks gently and softly. If you are reading the King James Version, it reads "a still small voice." That is the voice of God; he speaks in a still, small voice.

This is a very, very beautiful passage of Scripture. To give you the background of this story, Elijah was at a point in his life where he was very frustrated. He had fought so much; he had prophesied; he had battled so much against evil forces in the land. And at this point in his life, he was at a dead end. He'd had it, he was tired and frustrated. He felt he wasn't achieving much in his ministry; he felt he wasn't making much of a difference, and despite all the fights, the land was still in sin and people were still worshipping idols. Also his life was in danger; Jezebel the queen was after his life. Because of these frustrations, he needed to hear from God. He needed a confirmation that God was still behind him. He needed to know if God still cared for him. So he went to the mountain in the presence of the Lord and he was waiting for the Lord to come by and speak to him. All of a sudden there was a mighty rushing wind; the wind broke rocks into pieces and the stones were all over the place. Of course like any of us Elijah said, "This must be God." But the Bible says the Lord was not in the wind. As Elijah kept waiting, there came fire, then after that there was an earthquake, but the Bible says the Lord was not in any of them. Then later the voice of the Lord came in a gentle whisper. How often do we look for God in such dramatic manners? How often do we look to see God in some miraculous, extraordinary circumstances? How often do we look for God to appear in some unusual loud and noisy way? Until we understand God's nature, we might miss him like the prophet Elijah almost did.

The Bible says Elijah "pulled his cloak over his face." He didn't want to be distracted, because the voice is small. You need to make sure you kill everything that is noise around you. Psalm 46:10 says, "Be still, and know that I am God."

God speaks gently and softly. Oftentimes the noise around us would not allow us to hear him. There are two major sources of noise—two major kinds of noise, two major areas of our life where noise comes from—that need to be dealt with.

Two Sources of Background Noise

1. *The inside noise*

The first category is the noise on the inside. This is the noise in our mind. In order to hear God, our mind must be free of these noises. God relates to us by his Spirit, his Spirit relates to our human spirit. We have already said that as a man you are comprised of three parts; your spirit, soul, and body (see 1 Thessalonians 5:23). The most important of those parts is your spirit, because that is primarily who you are and the part of you that can connect with God. As a man you are a spirit that has a soul and lives in a body. In the Bible, the human spirit is also sometimes referred to as the inner man or inward man. Any time you come across the phrase *inner man*, the *inward man*, or the *spirit of a man* while reading the Bible, they are all referring to the same thing, which is the human spirit.

There is another part of you that is called the soul. The Bible commonly refers to the soul as the flesh or, simply, the mind. Sometimes it could also be referred to as the outward man (though outward man can also mean the physical body). This is very common when you read the Epistles of Apostle Paul. You will often see him using the phrase *outer man*, or *outward man*. He is talking about the soul. Your soul is comprised of your mind, your will, and your emotions. Your soul is where your mind, your will, and your emotions reside. Your soul is the center of your human nature and individual personality.

The third part the body, which is your physical body, is the house you live in. The body is also sometimes referred to as our outward man. See for example 2 Corinthians 4:16 NKJV: "Therefore we do not lose heart. Even though our outward man is perishing, yet the inward man is being renewed day by day."

When the Bible says, for example, "Love the Lord your God with all your heart and with all your soul and with all your strength" (Deuteronomy 6:5), it is speaking like that because those three are distinctive elements of our spiritual nature. Love God with your heart, which means your spirit; that is your inner man. Love God with your soul means in your mind, your will, and your emotions. Love God with your strength, or your body; that is your outermost man.

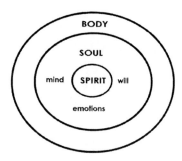

If you picture a man like three concentric circles (as shown above), your spirit is the nucleus, the innermost being; outside your spirit is the soul (which is comprised of mind, will, and emotions); and outermost is your body, your outermost being. When you get born again, your dead spirit is made alive through the Holy Spirit. The Holy Spirit forms a union with your spirit. One of the reasons why that union is formed is so God can communicate with you. Your regenerated spirit is turned into a receiver that can receive messages from God. Going back again to our analogy of how GPS receivers receive and process signals from the satellites, God activates your spirit by giving you the Holy Spirit and you are able to receive messages from God through the Holy Spirit (see Romans 8:9).

One of the major problems we have is that the human soul in its natural state is very noisy and loud. It is in our minds and emotions that we have strife, anger, jealousy, bitterness, worry, doubts, etc. These are all noises in our minds and emotions. They prevent us from hearing the voice of the Spirit of God speaking to our spirit. When two people are trying to communicate in a very noisy environment, it is always difficult for them to hear one another, especially when one of the parties only speaks gently. Whenever you are trying to communicate with someone in a very noisy environment, the natural thing is to begin to speak loudly to overcome the background noise so you can hear each other. In fact, if you stay long enough in the noisy place and later go outside that environment, you will find yourself speaking abnormally loud and people will start wondering what is wrong with you. I am sure we are all familiar with that picture. The problem is that God doesn't speak loudly; he speaks in a still, small voice. Hence people who have anger, bitterness, jealousy, strife, worry, and all those things will find it hard to hear him. Though it's alive, their spirit is living in a noisy environment.

There are also people who easily engage in murmuring and complaining. Those are noisy spirits—they have the spirit of murmuring and complaining. These kinds of people complain about life, complain about what God is doing in their life, they complain about whatever is going on around them. The children of Israel demonstrated this when they were in the wilderness (Numbers 14); they were always complaining. When God sent them manna from heaven, they complained. When the manna ceased, they complained. Sometimes we tend to be like the Israelites in the wilderness. We complain, "Why is that happening to me? Why can't my life be like this or that?" This kind of attitude creates a noisy environment for our spirit. If God wants to speak and tell you something, you can't hear him in that kind of atmosphere. You need to kill those background noises, because God speaks gently and softly.

Sometimes pride and arrogance are sources of noise in our mind. What is pride? It is the belief that you can figure it out by yourself. The spirit of pride is a very noisy spirit. How about stubbornness? Stubbornness is when we deliberately kick God out of certain areas of our lives. And sometimes we do that. We are so stubborn; we kick him out of an aspect of our life. Sometimes we kick God out of our relationships, our marriage. Some of us have kicked him out of our finances. No matter how he convicts you, no matter how he speaks to you, there is a spirit of stubbornness that deafens your spiritual ears. Your spirit can't hear because your mind is so noisy.

We all demonstrate that at some point in our lives. Sometimes we even demonstrate it visibly because that spirit doesn't want us to hear. Sometimes, even when the gentle voice of the Holy Spirit is speaking to your conscience, you just want to say, "No. Shut up. What do you know?"

Those are noisy things going on in our minds. Until we deal with these issues it is impossible to hear what God is saying. He wants to speak; in fact he is probably already speaking to you. When you have noise in the background, even though the signal is coming, it doesn't matter what the satellites are sending. As long as there is noise, you either don't hear at all or you don't hear correctly. You know that sometimes, even in a noisy environment, you can kind of read people's lips and somehow figure out what they are saying, but that is a very unreliable method of communication. You always tend to get messages that are inaccurate. There is always a great possibility of misunderstanding what is being said. The Bible says:

In quietness and trust is your strength.

—Isaiah 30:15

The reason why there is strength in quietness is because that is when you can accurately hear what God is saying. It takes a quiet spirit and mind to hear God accurately. Sometimes our prayer can even constitute noise when we don't spend some time in quietness.

I admire King David a lot; he was a man who was able to maintain a quiet spirit. Even though he was being persecuted, he was never living in anger or bitterness. That is why he was such a man that knew what God was saying. When there were issues in his life, this is what we learn that David did:

David inquired of the Lord, "Shall I pursue this raiding party? Will I overtake them?"

"Pursue them," he answered. "You will certainly over-take them and succeed in the rescue."

—1 Samuel 30:8

This is a very common occurrence in the life of David. He was a man that understood: "I can't entertain noise in my mind. I can't afford to have my spirit live in a noisy environment. I can't allow bitterness, strife, or anger to cloud my mind and prevent me from hearing what God is saying. The most important person I should listen to is God. If I hear what he is saying, I am confident." That is why we must always pray and ask God to help us to kill every loudness and every background noise going on in our mind.

Based on what we have said so far, your role as a believer is to make sure your soul is retrained to be quiet; that is why the Bible talks about renewing your mind. To renew means to retrain. The mind was originally created to be a quiet place, but that original nature was altered at the fall of man. When man ate from the tree of the knowledge of good and evil, the mind became overdeveloped. The soul became a noisy place; the soul became full of itself. Our responsibility as believers is to make sure that we retrain our soul through the Word of God. The daily reading, meditation, and confession of the Word of God help to retrain your mind.

There are so many things you stand to lose if you don't study and meditate on the Word of God. The Bible is not just a book of stories; the scriptures are not just verses you can use to pray, and they are not just stories to read so you can preach to people. No. The Bible is God's means of retraining your mind, renewing your mind, and refurbishing your mind, so it can return to the state of stillness and quietness where there is no more rowdiness and rebellion. This is very crucial to hearing the voice of God.

Apart from renewing your mind, you also need to strengthen your spirit, because your spirit is the host to the Holy Spirit. At creation, God's original intent was for the human spirit to be in charge. As a result of the Original Sin, our spirit became dead and our soul became overdeveloped, leading to a life controlled by the soul. At salvation the spirit of man is regenerated and is now in position to take charge. When the human spirit is in charge, God can be in charge, because he primarily relates with our spirit. But because the soul has been in charge for so many years, it won't give up the control easily. Hence your spirit needs to be strengthened, it needs to be able to stand up and talk to your soul and say, "Keep quiet, I am talking." Your spirit needs to be able to take charge. David's spirit was talking to his soul when he said, "Why are you cast down, O my soul? And why are you disquieted within me? Hope in God, for I shall yet praise Him" (Psalm 42:5 NKJV). The word *disquieted* means not quiet, it means troubled. The spirit wants to keep its hope in God, but the soul is just whining and complaining and talking. So the spirit spoke to the soul: "Keep quiet, hope in God." That was how David lived his life, and that is why he was such an accomplished man by all accounts.

However, only a strong spirit can do that. It is possible for our spirit to be alive but weak; sometimes the spirit has been weakened so much that it can't muster any strength to quiet our rowdy soul. Apostle Paul prayed for the Ephesian church that "he may strengthen you with power through his Spirit in your inner being" (Ephesians 3:16). He also says to the Corinthians, "A person who speaks in tongues is strengthened personally" (1 Corinthians 14:4 NLT). To be strengthened personally means to be strengthened on the inside. Hence we have a dual goal: to train our mind to be quiet and to strengthen our spirit. The Bible says that strengthening of our spirit also happens through the Word of God: "So then faith cometh by hearing, and hearing by the word of God" (Romans 10:17 KJV). When we study the Word of God, it renews the mind and strengthens our spirit to take charge.

Another way to quiet our soul is through worship. We learn that from the life of David—he was a worshipper. David was a man of so many troubles in his life. If you read about his life, you can't even imagine how he made it through all the uncertainties and the ups and downs he endured. For years he was afraid for his life. When he wasn't being hunted by King Saul, he was being hunted by his own son. In spite of all these troubles, he was a worshipper. Worship is how we bring serenity to our soul. Worship is also a form of prayer; prayer is a form of worship. That is why Philippians 4:6–7 says, "Do not be anxious about anything, but in every situation, by prayer and petition, with thanksgiving, present your requests to God. And the peace of God, which transcends all understanding, will guard your hearts and your minds in Christ Jesus." Your mind can experience that peace in prayer, worship, and thanksgiving.

Thanksgiving is the opposite of murmuring and complaining. When we live a life of worship and thanksgiving, our spirit and mind will experience peace and tranquility, which help us to hear that still, small voice. That is why it is usually in the process of worship that you know what God is talking about. When you give yourself to prayer and to worship, you know what God is saying.

Another way to quiet your mind is to practice simple obedience. Many of us quickly give in to the demand of our mind. Your spirit tells you, "Apologize to that person," but your mind says, "Why should I? It's not my fault?" Your spirit says gently, "It is good to apologize." Your mind shouts, "No!" Isn't that what we go through every day? Make that choice to say, "I will obey the voice of the Spirit." In your marriage, for example, make that choice to say, "My husband may not be the greatest guy in the world, but I will do what the Bible says. I will submit and let him have his way. Whatever he wants me to do, I'll do it." Or, "My wife may not be the greatest woman in the world, but I will love her and give myself to her regardless."

When you do this, you are training your mind. One thing you will notice in the first few instances is that your mind will protest and fight tooth and nail. This is because it was never used to that. After a few occasions the mind will get used to obeying the spirit. It will simply recognize that there is a new boss in town. It is like you are in a place of work and all of a sudden you are promoted among your peers to be the new manager. The first few months usually will be very rough, but after a few months, if you know what you are doing and demonstrate that you are truly in charge, everybody will begin to say, "You know what, there is a new boss in town, and you either follow suit or you are out." That is what obedience does. Small obedience leads to greater obedience. So also, small disobedience leads to greater disobedience. There is a dynamic that is going on between our spirit and our soul. Who is the boss? Our soul got an injection of rebelliousness when Adam ate the fruit, and thinks, "Now I can be the boss." But the soul is not a good leader. If you allow your soul to rule you, you will keep doing stupid and dumb things that you will keep regretting afterward. Any time you yield control of yourself to your mind, you have a greater tendency to do wrong things.

It always amazes me that when people do dumb things they say, "It is the devil." It is not the devil; it is really your own mind. People do dumb things and say, "It is the work of the devil." No. It is the work of your mind. You listened to your mind. Another powerful truth is that every little act of obedience always leads to greater obedience, because when you obey a little, the mind gets used to it and you can go a little farther in your obedience the next time. The more you obey, the easier it is to obey.

The same happens between your mind and your body, because the body is even worse than the mind. The farther you go outside the circle, the lesser the spiritual value. For example, you want to start exercising, your mind wants to exercise, the body says no. The first time you go to the gym, the body demonstrates by becoming very sore. Your legs become very sore and you experience pain all over your body. That is your body saying, "I don't want to do it." That is its own way of communicating. If you refuse to listen to your body and you continue to exercise, what happens? The body eventually gives in and begins to cooperate. The body realizes that you really want to do this and there is no amount of noise it can make that will make you stop, and it should just be quiet and cooperate. Hence the more you exercise, the easier it is to exercise.

2. The outside noise

The second category of noise is the outside noise. We have spent time talking about inside noise — everything going on in our inside. Now we are going to talk about the outside noise. Sometimes the greatest hindrances to hearing God are alternatives that the devil presents around us. Sometimes those alternatives can look quite good, but they are alternatives, they are not the real thing.

In Luke 10:38–42, there is a beautiful story of Mary and Martha that is very relevant to what we are talking about here. Jesus visited the house of these two precious, beautiful sisters. Jesus was a good friend with their brother, Lazarus, and became a very good family friend to all of them. Every time Jesus was in the area, he would stop by and pass the night or maybe even spend a few days in their house. On one of those occasions, while Jesus was sitting in the living room the Bible says Martha was busy with preparing food. She was running around, cooking, moving all over the place to make sure Jesus had something to eat. Mary, however, decided that the most important thing to her was what Jesus had to say to them; somehow she had rightly figured out that Jesus actually cares more about that. Maybe she had heard that on one occasion Jesus himself had said, "My meat is to do the will of him that sent me" (John 4:34 KJV). Or maybe she has heard Jesus said "As for everyone who comes to me and hears my words and puts them into practice, I will show you what they are like. 48 They are like a man building a house, who dug down deep and laid the foundation on rock." (Luke 6:47-48). So she knew Jesus doesn't really care too much about food. She figured that this little time I have with him; I better sit still and hear what he has to say and maybe ask him some questions. So the Bible says she sat with Jesus and was listening to Jesus.

Martha decided to be busy, running around trying to make some delicious dishes for Jesus to eat. At some point she became very overwhelmed and very upset. She stormed into the living room where Jesus and Mary were sitting, and she was not only mad at her sister, she was also mad at Jesus. She said, "Master, wouldn't you care? This girl should come and help me in the kitchen. I am busy running around and all she does is sit down with you here." Jesus replied, "Martha, you are too busy about too many things. You worry and fuss about a lot of things. You are too busy. There is one thing that I want. It looks like you have not really been paying attention to my sayings. I have visited you several times now, and I expected you to have understood who I am and what is more important to me. It looks like your younger sister is more attentive than you. She has chosen what is better, and it will not be taken away from her." Can you imagine how Martha must have felt? The Bible doesn't tell us, but I can just imagine how stupid she must have felt after Jesus said that, and you can't argue with Jesus.

Sometimes some of us can be too busy even for God, and sometimes we're even busy doing good things. Martha obviously felt that she was doing a good thing. She was serving, trying to give Jesus a splendid reception dinner. Sometimes we get busy running around taking care of our family. We get busy, so busy about life: the kids want to do this; we want to serve God; we want to organize this in the church. But we don't even find time to spend time in God's presence. We live in such a busy and noisy environment.

Sometimes it's the people we hang out with; we are surrounded by noisy people. Sometimes we talk too much. Some of us spend an awful lot of our time talking. Sometimes it is even our prayer that constitutes the noise. While you are praying and asking, God wants to speak to you, but you are just too busy praying. After a while God just stops trying. He says, "I want to answer you now. I want to say a word. I want to speak. But you won't let me."

Do you know why God gives us two ears and one mouth? Why didn't he give us two mouths? He gave us only one and I am glad he didn't give us two. He wants us to listen twice as much as we speak. Prayer is a dual-way communication. Communication with God is two-directional. We speak, and then he responds. God is always speaking. We should hear twice as much as speak. That is why King David said, "God has spoken once, Twice I have heard this: That power belongs to God" (Psalm 62:11 NKJV).

Have you ever been with people who just dominate the conversation? After a while you begin to feel irrelevant. You feel like your own opinion doesn't really interest them. In fact, after a while you don't want to be around them again because they won't allow you to talk. While they are talking, you listen, but as soon as you begin to talk they say, "I am sorry to cut you short" and they take over the conversation again. If you have any family or friends like that, you know how you feel about them. I think God feels like that sometimes because we are talking nonstop: "God, in the name of Jesus, do this and do that." But God is saying, "Please, let me say something." But you won't let him. Prayer can become noise when we don't listen to God. That is another example of outside noises.

Sometimes the outside noise is wrong counsel. That is why, again, David says, "Blessed is the one who does not walk in step with the wicked or stand in the way that sinners take or sit in the company of mockers," (Psalm 1:1). When you hang around the wicked, sinners, and mockers, you get a lot of wrong counsel that will constitute noise, preventing you from hearing the true Counselor.

It is great to have people around you who are in touch with God. Even when you want to do something wrong or stupid, they put you in check. They take you to the Word of God and say, "This is what the Word says about this situation." It is great to have people like that in your life. Unfortunately, many of us don't want that, because we just want noise.

> His sheep follow him because they know his voice. But they will never follow a stranger; in fact, they will run away from him because they do not recognize a stranger's voice.
>
> —John 10:4-5

If hearing God is so important to you, you would be willing to kill all the background noise. Sometimes, the problem is that we have not resolved, or we have not settled it in our minds, that hearing God is the most important thing. You need to be absolutely positive that hearing God is very important to you.

I love that song by the Christian group called Avalon: "I don't want to go somewhere/ If I know that You're not there." That should be your resolve as a believer. You should be able to say, "I don't want to do anything that displeases God, even if that thing appears profitable, popular, or acceptable to everyone around me" — sometimes that is an argument — "if in my heart I know God doesn't want it, even if everyone seems to be doing it." The Bible says, "Though hand join in hand, the wicked shall not be unpunished" (Proverbs 11:21 KJV). If everybody joins their hands and says, "We are going to do a wicked thing," it doesn't make the wicked thing more acceptable to God. When people are joining hands to do evil, you don't go in there because they are so many — God will still punish the wicked regardless of popularity or acceptance by the world.

In summary, to be able to hear God clearly, you must be willing to kill all the background noises inside and outside of you. It is also very important to note that the responsibility to kill the noises lies solely on you. It is not God's responsibility to kill the noises for you. Sometimes we expect God to do for us what he tells us to do. God is going to give us the grace, his grace is always available, but grace works where there is desire and willingnes to take initiative. We must take initiative to be still, we must take initiative to be quiet, and we must take initiative to remove those noises around us. We must also take initiative to move away from anything or anyone that constitutes noise around us. Then God will supply the grace to do so. Also, God is not going to speak louder to overcome the background noises in you or around you. He speaks in a still, small voice; you have to turn down the volume or leave the noisy environment so that you can hear what he is saying.

In quietness and trust is your strength, but you would have none of it.

— Isaiah 30:15

Chapter 8

Recalculating

If we confess our sins, he is faithful and just and will forgive us our sins and purify us from all unrighteousness.
—1 John 1:9

W hat I consider one of the best features of the GPS is the
ability to recalculate the direction to your destination
from another location during the course of your trip. This
is often needed, because most journeys end up not being as
straightforward as originally intended. I often say that if you
are one of those people who choose not to use GPS and stick
with Google Maps, MapQuest, or your old paper map, you can
do fine as long as you are a careful and attentive driver. If you
know how to drive and look at your map and pay attention to
the road signs at the same time, you will be fine. However all
these work fine until for some reason you miss your way or
things change along the way, which is fairly common. When
you are using a map and you miss your way or there is a road
block due to construction, things can get really complicated.
In those instances your map cannot easily help you. If you
have ever used a GPS, you will agree with me that one of best
values is revealed when you get lost or there is a detour or
road closure due to construction or accidents.

All GPS devices have a function called recalculating. It is
one of the most powerful and valuable functions of the GPS.
If you are driving and for some reason you turn left when
you are supposed to turn right, or somehow you miss your
exit on the highway or there is a road closure, your GPS can

recalculate your direction from a different location and give you an alternative direction to your destination. The function is built into all GPS devices. All of a sudden you hear your system saying "recalculating." In fact, you can judge the quality of your GPS device by how fast it recalculates. Some GPS receivers will take a while, and it will say "recalculating" like ten times, and you may have to park your car and stop for a while until it is done recalculating. The good ones will finish the process in a matter of a few seconds, without causing any delay or disruption in your trip.

The good news is that this process of recalculating is also applicable in our walk with God. Every day, whether we like it or not, we make choices, and there is always a chance that we make wrong choices. Even the best of us, the most spiritually alert of us, the most upright or the most in tune with God will make mistakes at some point in our lives. Because we are human, there is always a chance of making an error at some point in our lives. The good news is that God has addressed that possibility in his own GPS. He has his own "recalculating button" that you can always press and find your way back to him and to your destination. The great King David made reference to this when he said:

> As a father has compassion on his children, so the Lord has compassion on those who fear him; for he knows how we are formed, he remembers that we are dust.
>
> —Psalm 103:13–14

God in his infinite wisdom knows that even the best of us is still human and has the tendency to miss the mark at some point in our lives. Hence he has put a plan in place to ensure every miss does not result in missing our ultimate destination and purpose in life. Praise God, he is a God of second chances.

Maybe as you are reading this book you find yourself saying, "I wish I'd had this understanding ten years ago. I have made a lot of mistakes. I wish I had learned how to listen to God. Maybe I wouldn't have married this person. Maybe I wouldn't be here. Maybe I wouldn't be in the profession that I am. Maybe I would have made a lot of different choices than those I've made. I think that my life would have been been better off." Yes, all these might be true, but there is something that is truer: In Christ Jesus, with God's GPS you can always recalculate your way back to God's will.

The Bible tells us this: "And we know that in all things God works for the good of those who love him, who have been called according to his purpose" (Romans 8:28). Notice that this verse does not say only good things happen to those who love him. That is how we tend to read that passage sometime. The passage says in all things (good, bad or ugly) God works for the good of those who love him. There is a clear difference between the two statements. God can work out everything for your good. It doesn't matter how far you have gone, it doesn't matter how many mistakes you have made or wrong choices you have made or how far away you have detoured. In fact, God is so good at this that he can even convert our mistakes into blessings, if you can press that recalculate button. If you can just say, "God, I am willing to do what you want now", it doesn't matter how far you have gone, there is always a way back—quicker than you think—to where God wants to take you.

To illustrate this, I don't think there is a better story than the story Jesus himself told us in the book of Luke, chapter 15. This is one of the most popular parables of Jesus Christ in the bible, generally referred to as the parable of the prodigal son or parable of the lost son. Speaking in parables is one of the remarkable things about Jesus' teaching ministry. A parable is simply a story that illustrates a truth. This method of speaking became one of the distinctive marks of Jesus' style of teaching. Anytime he wanted to communicate a powerful truth, he would usually start by telling a story and then go into the point he was making. Sometimes he would say a parable in response to a question especially when he wants to make a larger point than the question. The parable has a way of getting people curious and interested in the subject. People start wondering, "What is he driving at? What is he trying to say?"

Jesus was a very interesting person to listen to. One thing I love about Jesus is that he was never a boring speaker. He was very creative, compelling, relevant, captivating, and effective.

I wish a lot of preachers were more like Jesus. Let us begin the parable of the prodigal son:

> Jesus continued: "There was a man who had two sons. The younger one said to his father, 'Father, give me my share of the estate.' So he divided his property between them."

—Luke 15:11–12

Here is a story of a father who had two sons; the youngest son happened to be a little bit more aggressive. He is the kind of a guy who takes things into his own hands a little bit, so he came up with an idea: I think I should leave home and get out of this place. I should be able to do better on my own. So he went to the father and said, "Give me my own share of the inheritance."

In the Jewish culture, it is customary for a man to leave an inheritance for his children. Abraham left an inheritance for Isaac, and Isaac left inheritance for Jacob. In fact King Solomon actually said, "A good person leaves an inheritance for their children's children" (Proverbs 13:22). So it was the culture in those days, and because of that everybody understood what Jesus was saying. The difference is that this guy decided to get his inheritance it a little early. He wasn't willing to allow the father to die. He said, "I am sure you have a plan; I am sure you have set up an account for us. Why don't you give me my portion of that plan now, so I can begin to enjoy it early?" He presented that brilliant idea to the father.

The other son decided, "I am going to stay here." So you see two people who made two different choices. Every day we have a chance to make choices, we make choices as to whether to stay in God's will or to go outside of it. Whether you are in God's will or not is always a question of choice. There are some Christians who have bought into some weird schools of thought that God is responsible for everything that happens to them. For these people anything that happens to them is God. Even when they make bad choices, they will still attribute them God. They say, "It was God who made me make that choice." You can imagine a guy who is low on gas in his car but is too lazy and mindless to stop by at the nearest gas station. Then he runs out of gas and says, "Praise God. God actually has a plan for this. He wanted me to run out of gas and get stuck on the highway so I can learn some perseverance." In fact, sometimes a guy like that would say, "I know God arranged this one because I was able to preach the gospel to the driver of the towing vehicle that came to tow my car." The truth is that he could have stopped by at the gas station early and preached the gospel to the guy at the gas station too. God is not responsible for our bad choices.

There is another school of thought that believes the devil is responsible for everything that happens. For people who subscribe to this ideology, anything that happens to them they say, "The devil made me to do it." I am sure the devil is sometimes tempted to go to God and say, "This is not me. I know I do a lot of bad things, but this one I didn't do." If the devil is so powerful that he can make everybody do what he wants, many believers would not be alive today. In fact, no preacher would be alive. The truth is that the devil is not as powerful as we think.

The more balanced and scriptural truth is to accept that we are all largely products of our decisions. It is our decisions that create our circumstances. Every day we are presented with opportunities to make choices to stay in the will of God or to go outside of it. This younger son decided, "I want to take my inheritance as go outside of God's will." He made that choice.

That brings me to an interesting question. Why did the father comply? Why did the father say, "You want it? I give it to you." Why didn't he do what my own dad would have done? My own dad would have said, "What is wrong with you? Are you out of your mind?" This is what I think Jesus is driving at: God does not operate by forcing us to do his will. The Bible says he has called us into a life of freedom.

> You, my brothers and sisters, were called to be free. But do not use your freedom to indulge the flesh; rather, serve one another humbly in love.
>
> —Galatians 5:13

God doesn't operate by force; instead he gives us a choice. He wants us to obey him because we want to, not because we have to. God wants us to do what he wants because we also want it, not because we have to. The Bible says he actually works in us to will and to do his pleasure (see Philippians 2:13). He doesn't want us to be robots; robots have no will, they only do what they are told to do. That is why God is interested in both our willingness and obedience. If not for that attribute, he could have forced the son to stay. He could have said, "I am your father. No matter what you do, you are not leaving this house." He can also threaten him and say, "If you leave this house, you forfeit all your inheritance." God doesn't do that. God created us as free moral agents. He gave us free will and encourages us to use that will rightly. That is why he told the Israelites, "I have set before you life and death, blessings and curses. Now choose life, so that you and your children may live" (Deuteronomy 30:19).

That is why a lot of times, when we want to do dumb things, God doesn't say, "I am not going to let you do it." When we want to go our own way, even though it is painful for him, God says, "Okay, if that is what you want to do." I can imagine how painful this is for the father in this parable. I have to imagine it is painful for the father to see his son just abandon him like that, but he said, "You can." The Bible says he divided his property and gave a portion to his son. Let me bring out another point here, the fact that God has not been forcing you doesn't mean he is happy with the choices you are making. Some of us want to commit some sin or want to do something that we know is wrong and we say, "If God can allow me to do it, if he doesn't stop me from doing it, then I am okay." No, the father doesn't act like that. The fact that he doesn't strike you every time you make a wrong choice doesn't mean he is happy with your choice. The Bible says that when we come before him with idols in our hearts, he will answer us according to the idol in our hearts (see Ezekiel 14:3–4). If I really want something and I go to God and say, "Lord, I want this from you," but he whispers gently and says, "Son, this is not good for you." If I still continue to press him for it, he may simply say, "Okay, you can have it" even though he is not interested in me having it.

This happened when the children of Israel were looking for a king (see 1 Samuel 8). They went to Samuel and said, "Let's forget about this idea of having a prophet for our president. We don't look good as a country. How can we compete in the world stage like that? It doesn't look good for us as a nation to have a clergy as a leader; in fact, people are making fun of us. Are we that dumb? Let us have a real president." Samuel said, "It is not good for you. You are different; you are not like those other nations. God wants to be your president." They said to Samuel, "I don't think you understand us. When we go to world organizations, people are laughing that our president is a prophet with a beard and he is saying 'praise the Lord' when he wants to talk. It doesn't look good."

God then said, "Okay. If that is what you want, go choose them someone. But let me tell you: Your king is going to oppress you. If you choose to have a king, that means you are actually rejecting me as your king. If you have your own king, he is going to oppress you. He is going to use your sons as his slaves. He is going to take your wives. He is going to do whatever he wants to you." They said, "Okay, as long as we look good." They had it. The story was not very nice after that. That is any example of pressuring God to say yes when he already said no.

It happens to us every time. When we want to make a bad choice, God gently says, "Please, don't do this; don't make this choice." But we insist and say, "God I want to do this, please approve it." Sometimes if we pray hard enough the prayer gets answered, not because the request is God's will but because he is leaving us to our will. For example, if you pray so hard about marrying someone, God can say, "Okay. Marry him, or marry her." That doesn't mean that he is really approving your choice. He is simply answering you according to the idol in your heart. That is why the greatest prayer that we can pray is "God, let your will be done." Let's go on with our story:

Not long after that, the younger son got together all he had, [and] set off for a distant country.

—Luke 15:13

Now the story is getting interesting. As soon as the younger son got his inheritance, he allowed a few weeks to pass by and decided to relocate to another city that is far away. The Bible doesn't say why he decided to relocate after that, but I think I can guess. The whole reason behind all his moves is that he was tired of living under his father's rules. He wanted freedom, he wanted independence. Isn't that why we all run away from God? He wanted to be free; he wanted to be able to do what he wanted. "As long as I am in Daddy's house, there is a curfew; he tells me I must be home by 9:00 p.m. He tells me who can visit me. He tells me what I can do. I have some friends with wonderful parents; their parents don't put all these kinds of restrictions on them."

I remember I used to feel like that when I was younger. "Why can't my dad be like some of my friends' dads? My dad tells me I have to be home by 7:00 p.m. I have to read for two hours before I can go and play soccer with my friends. I can't watch TV until certain times. What kind of dad is this?" I use to tell my friends, "Man, I wish my dad was like your dad." I don't wish that anymore. I thank God that my dad was the way he was to me when I was younger. I suspect this was the prodigal son's problem; he was tired of the father's rules. He was tired of the restrictions that he felt when he was with his dad.

It could also be that he wanted to explore. "Let me just know what is going on out there in the world." A lot of young people who are Christians have the tendency to think like that. They say to themselves, "This Christianity is shielding me; this relationship with God is limiting me in many areas. I want to know what is going on out there. I can always come back home after. I will come back to faith, don't worry, Mommy; I am not going too far. I just want to have some life experience." Unfortunately, by the time they come back, they come back with scars and bruises. They come back badly beaten. After they come back they have to spend many years to clean up all the mess in their lives. The truth is, it is better never have those kind experiences and messes than to have to get over them. Maybe that was the issue the prodigal son had. Sometimes people say to themselves, "I think I want to explore and enjoy life a little. I want to have some stories to tell when I grow old." You don't need those kinds of stories. There are some stories that you don't need in your life.

There is one thing you have to admit about this young boy: He was a smart kid. He wanted to have it both ways. He valued and wanted the father's wealth, but he didn't want a relationship with the father. He wanted the possessions without the obligations and the responsibilities of a relationship. That is the attitude many of us have toward God today. This is the reason why many of us are not in his will, the reason we find it easy to stray—it's because we value what he can offer, but we don't want the obligation of a real relationship with him. That is why we all pray when we are in need and why some of us go to church only when we are going through something—we value what he has, we value what he can do but not his presence. We want to keep him at arm's length, close enough to collect his blessings but not close enough for a meaningful relationship.

That is why I think the church leaders are doing a lot of disfavor to the members. You have all these churches that say they specialize in breakthrough prayer. When you go there, what are they praying about? It is all about "God, do this for me." Everything is for me or against my enemy. Those are the only two things they are talking about. Gather a prayer meeting together that is focused on kingdom purpose, gather a prayer meeting together that is focused on spiritual development, and you won't see many people. If they do come, after a while they will start asking, "When are we really going to start the prayer?" Sometimes people call me and ask, "Does your church have night vigil service or does your churh have special breakthrough sevice?" I know what they are talking about. I say, "Every service is a breakthrough service." Nothing is wrong with night vigils or breakthrough service, but a lot of times I know what they are really asking for. "When are we going to really pray about blessings, breakthroughs and all those good stuff?"

I have discovered that a lot of times people want the gifts, but they don't want the giver. They do not necessarily say verbally that they don't want him, but their actions show that they don't want to keep him too close for their comfort. Sometimes they might show some respect for him. They might go to church regularly as long as it is convenient. They might even join a ministry and *serve*. But fundamentally, a lot of believers don't want to submit to God's authority. If you look seriously into their lives, if you look at what is driving them, it is not a genuine desire to submit to God. They are dealing with God at arm's length. They don't want his rules in their lives. They don't want the apparent restrictions that walking with God might bring. They want his blessing, but not the responsibility of a relationship.

I want to ask you at this juncture, are you making the same mistake in your life? How do you deal with God in your marriage challenges? Do you fundamentally want to do what God wants, or do you want God just to resolve the marriage problem? Are you just saying, "Please, God, just bring peace into my marriage." Or are you willing to submit to his will concerning what he says in that marriage? Peace will come if we are willing to submit to him.

Are you having challenges in your finances? How do you deal with God in your finances? Are you just saying, "Lord, bless me, bless me. O Lord, bless me, give me money." Or are you fundamentally willing to submit to him in the area of your finances? When things get tough, when bills are mounting, what is the first thing to do? Is God the first person you go to? That is how you know what is driving you fundamentally. How do you deal with him in all aspects of your life and in the choices you make?

As a single Christian man or woman, what choices are you making in the area of sexual purity? Do you find it easy to compromise? If you are in a relationship, are you making excuses to have sex before marriage? Are you saying, "Well, we are going to marry each other anyway?" That is an excuse to compromise your faith. That is the problem the prodigal son had. In many ways, the church of nowadays resembles the prodigal son. He wanted the blessing, he wanted the good, but he didn't want a serious relationship God.

Let me ask you a question. What do you really want? Do you want God or do you just want his stuff? That is a good question to ask. Do you want him or do you just want his stuff? Do you want whatever you can get out of him while you keep him at arm's length? Is that your purpose? If that is what is fundamentally driving you, you can't stay in his will. Let's go on with the story:

> "… and there squandered his wealth in wild living [unconstrained living, which is what he wanted]. After he had spent everything, there was a severe famine in that whole country, and he began to be in need."

> —Luke 15:13–14

Getting away from God's will, no matter how thrilling it is at the beginning, always lead to a life of no fulfillment. It will always end you up in a life or a place of emptiness. The Bible says, "There is a way that appears to be right, but in the end it leads to death." (Proverbs 14:12). No matter how exciting it is, it will always end up with a famine. That is exactly what happened to this boy. After he severed the relationship with his father, he began to enjoy wild living without constraints, without anybody telling him what to do or not to do anymore, but we see what happened with him. He ended up in emptiness.

> "So he went and hired himself out to a citizen of that country, who sent him to his fields to feed pigs."

> —Luke 15:15

He did what many of us would do after we have messed up. This is very natural after people have gone away from God and they begin to feel that emptiness. And soon we begin to sense, "It looks like this thing is backfiring," instead of recalculating the GPS and returning back to God, we try to solve the problem somehow on our own. We try to figure it out first without involving God. We say, "What can I do? What other options are out there for me?" In the parable of the prodigal son, the prodigal son "went and hired himself out to a citizen of that country." He was far away from God now, he has been hanging out with guys that his father wouldn't have appoved of and it has backfired on him. He went and hired himself out and he began to feed pigs. He began to work for them. Let me ask you, where is the freedom that he wanted now? If you start working for someone, don't they tell you when to come to work? If you start working for someone, don't they tell you when to stand up? Don't they tell you what you can do and what you caint? In his pursuit of freedom outside of his father house, this guy ended up in real slavery. Worse still, it is slavery to people who don't really like him and have his interest at heart. If you want to be a slave, at least be a slave to someone who is nice, who really likes you and has your interest at heart. Unfortunately that is not what happened to the prodigal son. Out of desperation, he hired himself out to strangers.

> "He longed to fill his stomach with the pods that the pigs were eating, but no one gave him anything."

> —Luke 15:16

As you go further in the story you discover that things actually got worse for the prodigal son. You begin to realize that he probably wasn't even getting paid or wasn't paid well enough. He started the job, payday came and they said, "We are sorry, we didn't make enough money." Then this guy started to eat with the pigs. That is what happens to you when you leave the father's house. Maybe you are in that situation; you have walked away from the father. You have made wrong choices. Maybe God even warned you. He might have used people around you to warn you. Maybe God himself told you that what you are doing is wrong, that where you are going is nowhere. God's GPS said, "Turn left." But you went straight. Then the GPS recalculated and said, "Make a U-turn and go back to make a right." But you keep on going straight. After a while the GPS would say, "You can go wherever you want to go."

If you have made those wrong choices and it has backfired on you, my advice is don't go farther away. Don't say, "It has backfired, but now I have to figure it out on my own. I don't want church people or my parents to have the last laugh on me." Forget about people laughing at you; you should care more about being in God's will for your life. The same people that knew our prodigal son and envied him while he was in his father's house are now employing and enslaving him. It is even possible that he had looked down on some of them while he was in his father's house. Isn't it sad that the same devil that you have bound and cast out is now the one controlling your life. That is not God's will for you, and you can change that in Jesus' name!

Can you imagine that the same devil that you told, "I walk on your head, in the name of Jesus," is now the boss when you walk away from God? He is now the one controlling you. Some of us, the same unbelievers living in sin that you preached to in the past, are now the ones dictating how your life will be. That is what happened to this guy. The use of the word *pigs* by Jesus here is very deliberate. You can't catch a Jewish guy with a pig. Pigs are considered impure and an abomination in the Jewish culture. They can't eat pig; they can't even touch it. Even in the New Testament pigs are associated with demons.

Have you ever seen pigs? It is possible that you don't know much about pigs. I know pigs because some of my uncles were pig rearers. When I was a kid growing up in southwestern Nigeria, my family used to travel to my mom's hometown far out in the country for holidays. Some of my uncles bred and reared pigs, and we would sometimes go to the pig farm. The pig farm, especially in an African village, is not a pretty place to be. It is a place where people dump all kinds of nasty garbage. People throw their feces, rotten food, and all kinds of things there, and that is what the pigs feed on. I can imagine that the pig farm in the first-century Jewish village would be similar to that. It gets so bad for the prodigal son that he was eating with the pigs. That is absolute desperation. I can imagine his reasoning was, "I can't go back to my father. It will be a great shame; other kids in the house will be laughing at me. I can't take that; I have to figure it out." That was his reasoning, until, as we see in verse 17, things got so bad it became practically unbearable. He was now at his wit's end, having tried everything he could to survive without his father. He has tried everything possible not to have to go back home and say "Sorry" to his father. Then he realized his foolishness and changed his thinking.

> "When he came to his senses, he said, 'How many of my father's hired servants have food to spare, and here I am starving to death!"

> —Luke 15:17

Notice how he changed his reasoning and started talking differently to himself here. Sometimes we need to do exactly that; change our reasoning and talk to ourselves. That is what the Bible calls repentance. The prodigal son continues:

> I will set out and go back to my father and say to him: Father, I have sinned against heaven and against you. I am no longer worthy to be called your son; make me like one of your hired servants.'

> —Luke 15:18–19

He reasoned to himself and said, "I think it is better to be a servant in my father's house than to be out here. Even servants in my father's house have good food and a decent place to sleep. They may not have an inheritance, but at least they have what they need for now. It is better to be ashamed in my father's house than to be living like this." He recalculated his way back home. In God's GPS, that is what it means to press the recalculate button. He said, "I know I have gone too far, but there is always a way back home." That is what I am challenging you to do. I don't know where you have swerved from God's purpose for your life. Maybe not too long after you turned, you realized you made a mistake, but you still kept on going anyway, thinking, "I will just figure my way out." Why don't you just press that recalculate button and come back to God? Look at what the Bible says:

If we claim to be without sin, we deceive ourselves and the truth is not in us. If we confess our sins, he is faithful and just and will forgive us our sins and purify us from all unrighteousness.

—1 John 1:8-9

Even the best of us go astray once in a while. The Bible says that anyone who says "I am perfect" is a liar. Anyone who kept going anyway even after realizing that they had made the wrong turn is living in deception. The good news is that verse 9 above says there is always the recalculate button. Faithfulness is God's attribute; it is actually a rare attribute among men. God is a faithful God, and I am glad the promise of forgiveness depends on his faithfulness and not on ours. He forgives us and restores us because of himself, not because of us. God has his own integrity to uphold. He is faithful; he cannot make himself unfaithful. Why would God ever do that? He is not just faithful to forgive us but also to cleanse us. Cleansing means restoration. Forgiveness means he is not counting your error or your sin against you anymore. Restoration goes further than that; it means he is restoring everything you have lost in the process of going away, whether it is financial, relationships, peace, joy, or even time. It means God is saying, "I can bring you back to the state you were in before you left, maybe even better." Praise God for his faithfulness.

The Bible also says this in another portion: "Turn you to the strong hold, ye prisoners of hope: even to day do I declare that I will render double unto thee" (Zechariah 9:12 KJV). Sometimes God says, "I can even give you double for your trouble if you are willing to say, 'Lord, I am recalculating back; Lord, I am coming back. I know I have made a lot of bad choices and I am very sorry for that. I know I have gone far away but please forgive me. I wish I had read this book ten, five, or two years ago but now I am turning back to God anyway." Forget about what has happened. *Now* you can turn and find your way back to him.

The prodigal son says to himself, "I am going to try. I am going to plead. I know he may not restore me to the status of his son again, but I will just apply if I can be a servant there." However, on the other end at home, there is a different thing going on in the father's mind. When the son was leaving, the father's feeling was not that of anger but of sadness. That is exactly how God feels about us when we go astray. Sometimes we think, "God is so mad at me, if he ever catches me, I am in trouble." That is how we feel about him because many of us have earthly fathers who are like that, but God's feeling is different.

As long as his son was away, the father was always unhappy. Sometimes the servants or the other son would observe the father's countenance and ask him what was wrong. He would reply, "It's my son, I miss my son. I wish he had never made that bad choice. I wish he never walked away. I wish he had listened to me. I pray he finds his way back home. I want him back. I am hoping one day he will come to his senses. I am hoping he realizes there is still a place for him here." That is how the father was feeling. Notice how different that is from the son's perception. The prodigal son misjudged his father's feelings because he said, "There is no way he is taking me back. Forget about taking me back, the best I can hope for is to be admitted back as a servant. I know at least some people work for him, and I will apply and tell him, 'Just pretend you don't know me. Just hire me just like you hire other people.' "

However, the Bible says the father was always looking outside. Anytime he saw a car pull into the driveway he thought it was his son, anytime he saw someone walking toward the house, he would jump up and look to see if that was his lost son coming back home. The father saw him from afar because he was looking. He had been hoping for this day for a long time. Hence the Bible says as soon as the man saw him he ran toward him. That is the only time God ran in the Bible. There is no other place running is attributed to God in the Bible. Every time posture or movement is attributed to God, he is either standing, sitting, walking, or watching. That is his posture. The only time he ran was toward that boy who was lost and recalculated his steps back.

GPS – God's Positioning System

The Bible says the father ran toward him, hugged him, and kissed him. I can imagine servants saying to themselves, "Is this man okay? Here is a boy who messed up really bad, and even if you are going to hug him, shouldn't you first give him some real scolding? After which you can then say, 'Let's talk.' Our boss is such a weak man." Even the older son was quite disappointed at the father's overt display of joy at this undeserving rebellious boy. Later he came to the father and said, "What is going on?" and the father said, "My son that was lost is found; he was dead and is alive again." That is how God responds when we run back to him in repentance. The fact is nobody comes to God in repentance only to hear him say, "You don't deserve it" or "I have to punish you before I accept you." The Catholic Church has a concept called purgatory, which generally implies that before God accepts people he puts them somewhere where they have to suffer for a while before they are accepted. That concept is not the picture the Bible gives us of God. Here is how how the bible describes the follow-up reaction of the father

> "But the father said to his servants, 'Quick! Bring the best robe and put it on him. Put a ring on his finger and sandals on his feet. Bring the fattened calf and kill it. Let's have a feast and celebrate. For this son of mine was dead and is alive again; he was lost and is found.' So they began to celebrate.

> — Luke 15:22-24

There is always a celebration in heaven whenever anyone who went away comes back to God in repenetance.

I would like to touch briefly on the issue of older son's reaction. Just like any other person, he was mad at what he apparently considered a display of disregard or unfair treatment by the father toward him.

> "The older brother became angry and refused to go in. So his father went out and pleaded with him. But he answered his father, 'Look! All these years I've been slaving for you and never disobeyed your orders.

102

Yet you never gave me even a young goat so I could celebrate with my friends. But when this son of yours who has squandered your property with prostitutes comes home, you kill the fattened calf for him!'

"'My son,' the father said, 'you are always with me, and everything I have is yours. But we had to celebrate and be glad, because this brother of yours was dead and is alive again; he was lost and is found.' "

—Luke 15:28–32

Can you see how he feels? He was so mad that he wouldn't even go in; he considered the father's celebration about the younger son's return as an insult to him. He said, "What is wrong with Dad? What do you see in this boy that warrants all this excessive display of joy and partying? What did we miss about him while he was gone? How important is he? Why are you running after him?" There are many ways we can interpret this action, but the fact is, God's grace does not make sense to human senses. From a human-reasoning point of view, God's grace is not fair and there will always be people around you who would think you don't deserve it. I have even seen this happen in church. Oftentimes when someone has sinned or erred openly and then come back in repentance, there are people who feel that such a person doesn't deserve to be accepted back into fellowship or at least not that soon. Sometimes this prevalent attitude in church can affect the prodigal believers and discourage them from coming back to fellowship. Knowing that people around them might react like the older brother might hinder them from coming back. Some of these concerns are genuine; I believe the older brother was also genuine, only he was genuinely wrong. Sometimes the hindrance to your recalculation process might actually be from people you don't expect. However, from this parable we have learned that the most important feeling is that of the father. Sometimes the greatest sources of hindrance to someone coming to Jesus are actually the folks closest to Jesus who are supposed to know better. In their sincerity, it was the disciples who sent little children away from Jesus (Matthew 19:13–15), it was also the disciples who tried to discourage the woman with the alabaster box from pouring its contents on Jesus, an action that Jesus greatly commended (Matthew 26:6–13). In each of these cases, Jesus sided with the person trying to come to him against those blocking access to him.

Another point here is that grace extended to one person does not imply grace taken away from another. The father said to the older brother, "All I have is yours." This implies that if it had been him in the same situation, he would have been treated the same way. What a powerful truth we can learn here. When it comes to his grace, God is not a respecter of person. God's resources are unlimited. Only people with limited resources get mad at any apparent wastage of it. God has so much that it is not a big deal. The father said, "Let's kill a cow. Let's have a party. Let's have fun. Let's enjoy because my son has come back to his senses." That is the most important issue to this father and also to our heavenly father.

You may be wondering, "What is the basis of God's forgiveness, why is he this generous and so forgiving? Why is he even willing to go as far as restoring everything lost in the process?" The answer is very simple: It is Jesus Christ of Nazareth. The sacrifice of Jesus Christ on the cross of Calvary is the basis of our being forgiven, accepted, and restored.

> God presented Christ as a sacrifice of atonement, through the shedding of his blood — to be received by faith. He did this to demonstrate his righteousness, because in his forbearance he had left the sins committed beforehand unpunished.
>
> — Romans 3:25

When we go to God in repentance, he forgives not because we are deserving of his forgiveness but because someone already paid for it by offering his life for our sins and wrongdoing. It is also important to know that when you go back to God, the only basis upon which you can go is through Jesus Christ. The fact is that God already gave us the most anyone can at redemption; hence he will not refuse us any access to him when we go back to him in sincerity. He who did not spare his own Son, but gave him up for us all—how will he not also, along with him, graciously give us all things? (See Romans 8:32.)

I don't know in what area of your life you feel you have messed up and need the grace and forgiveness of God. If you want to press that recalculate button, just tell it to him. Don't hide anything from him; just tell him, "Lord, I have missed it in this area. I have ignored you and have gone my own way." He is your father and you don't need to be cute with him. You don't need to be fancy or dress up the issue with him. Just tell him, "God, I have missed it. I have abandoned your will and have gone my own way, but now I have come to my senses and I want to come back. Please restore me. I know you are faithful; I know you are just. Forgive me, cleanse me, and restore me in the name of your son Jesus Christ. Amen."

Chapter 9

It's Personal

You have searched me, Lord, and you know me. You know when I sit and when I rise; you perceive my thoughts from afar. You discern my going out and my lying down; you are familiar with all my ways.

—Ephesians 1:11-12

I have observed that when it comes to teaching about hearing from God, it is all too common for church people to quickly rush into methods and manners. I have heard teacher after teacher teaching on how God speaks while primarily emphasizing one method after the other. Some talk about dreams, visions, audible voices, inner witness, etc. If you have noticed, I have carefully stayed away from methods in this book. That is because I am convinced that when it comes to dealing with God and hearing from God it is more of a relational matter than a doctrinal one. Doctrines and principles are good; they give us a structure, an approach, and an easy starting point in our dealing with God, but they are not the real issue. Unfortunately it is so easy in the body of Christ to get so hung up on doctrines and methods. When it comes to praying, for example, it helps to know that we must ask in the name of Jesus, start with worship and thanksgiving, and make sure we confess our sins. Those are good doctrinal issues and principles. However, I want to submit to you that real, powerful, and effective prayer life can only be developed out of a personal relationship with God. In the same manner, it is very hard for someone to teach you methods of listening to your father. If I have a father, after living with him for some time, I know what his winking means. I can even decode his certain looks. Some of us growing up with mom; you know what she means when she looks at you in some manner. You know what she really means when she speaks to you with certain tones. You instinctively know what she is saying. A stranger would not be able to understand it, but you know that, "When Mom looks at me this way, she is not happy with what I am doing."

It is exactly the same way with hearing from God; the emphasis should be on relationship. It is not difficult to know what God is saying when your goal is really to attain a father and child relationship. That is the whole essence of this book. You will notice that in the Bible, Jesus always meets people at the point of their needs. He is very personal in his approach with people. When it comes to dealing with God, there are principles that apply, but the heart of the matter is a solid, personal relationship with him. The insurance companies like to talk about group rate, which is when everybody gets the same rate because they belong to a group. With hearing God, there is nothing like group rate, everything is personal. I once heard a commercial by a car dealership on one of the radio stations in New Jersey; they came up with what is called "in-person pricing." That means the price we give you is for *you*, based on your particular financial situation and your need. In some ways God is like that when it comes to hearing him; he is up close and personal and he deals with you based on who you are and where you are.

Jesus demonstrated this in several ways while he was here. In John chapter 4, when he met the woman at the well, the conversation was personal. He started with her from the place she was in her journey of life and invited her into a higher place with him. It was this personal conversation that transformed the life of that woman and the entire city of Samaria.

In John chapter 5, Jesus met the crippled man by the pool in Bethesda and asked, "Do you want to get well?" and the conversation begins about the challenges the man was facing that had prevented him from getting healed until then. He said, "When the pool rises, I have nobody to carry me." The conversation ended with, "Get up! Pick up your mat and walk." Jesus met that man where he was and changed his life forever.

Also, in Mark 8:22–25, when they brought him the blind beggar, he didn't just heal him; he took him by the hand and led him outside the village. He then spit on the man's eyes and put his hands on him. When the man could not see well after the first attempt, Jesus put his hands again on his eyes until he could see everything clearly. This is Jesus being personal. Two chapters later, in Mark 10:46–52, he was approached by another blind man. While everyone was telling the blind man to be quiet, Jesus stopped the crowd and asked them to bring him. He asked him, "What do you want me to do for you?" The blind man said, "Rabbi, I want to see." Jesus said, "Your faith has healed you." And immediately the man received his sight. Two men with the same problem of blindness, but Jesus approached their healing differently based on where they were in life.

The same is true when he met Zacchaeus, the chief tax collector (Luke 19:1–10). Jesus got to the spot under the sycamore tree branch he was on, then he looked up and said to him, "Zacchaeus, come down immediately. I must stay at your house today." That is Jesus being personal. "I need to have lunch with you so you can know who I am." It was the same with Matthew the tax collector (Matthew 9:9–12). Jesus went to his office and asked him to follow him. He later had dinner at Matthew's house with many of his friends.

In the same way, we all come to Jesus as unique individuls with unique circumstances, challenges, personalities, backgrounds, and places in life. Yet God deals and speaks with each of us in ways peculiar to us in order to navigate us to the place of his purpose and plan for us. That is why I would like to repeat again here: The most important issue is not about learning the methods but developing and maintaining a dynamic personal relationship with him. There is no method that I can tell you that will be more important than this. If I begin by telling you, "God speaks this way or that way," I would be doing a disservice to him, because he is just too personal to be stereotyped or boxed into a corner. My sense is, as you begin to develop a relationship with God and nurture your desire to know him, you will figure that one out.

I want you to understand that I am not trying to knock down any of the methods you have heard. I am only saying that focus on methods is putting the cart before the horse. I am sure you have heard of different methods and means through which God speaks. Yes, you have heard right: God speaks through audible voices and inner witness of the spirit. He sometimes speaks using other people, and he can also use situations and circumstances. God can speak to you while reading his Word or while listening to a message in church. He also speaks through prophecies, visions, and dreams. Sometimes opened and closed doors can be God speaking to you, and sometimes God's will can be as simple as sanctified common sense. The problem is that emphasizing any of these methods can lead to overattachment to them, which in turn leads to a lot of errors and demonic manipulations. For example, I have seen many believers who take the issue of dreams too far. They believe every dream they have is God speaking to them and try to find interpretations for them somehow. When the truth is that most people over the age of ten dream at least four to six times per night, and most of the dreams are just mundane "doodles" taken from the events of our lives. This is not to say God doesn't speak to us through dreams, but the truth is, he does so only sparingly.

I have also seen a group of believers who take the issue of inner witness and audible voice of the Holy Spirit as far as saying that you cannot claim to be saved until you hear an audible voice of the Holy Spirit literarily telling you that you are now a child of God. They base this belief on Romans 8:16, which says, "The Spirit himself testifies with our spirit that we are God's children." So you find people in this group praying and waiting to be saved for one, two, or three years, because they were taught, "You are not saved yet until you hear the voice." A careful reading of Romans 8:16 in context will show you that this passage is talking about the need to walk and live by obeying the Spirit and is not necessarily a prescription on how to hear the voice of God. Don't get me wrong, God speaks through the audible voice, but a careful study of the Scriptures will show you that it is not such a common occurrence.

Emphasis on these methods has a way of idolizing them and taking our focus away from the most important issues, which are: a real relationship with God, a life of surrender, sacrifice, and continuous renewal of our mind. When those are the focus of a believer, knowing God's will becomes easy and a natural result. However, as I have mentioned before now, principles can serve as a general guide and as a starting point to hearing God, and we are going to take a look at some of these principles that can be very helpful as we seek to know God and hear his voice.

The Word of God Is God Speaking to You

The Bible is not a storybook, though it contains a lot of stories. Neither is it a history book, though it is historical in nature. The Bible in not just prophecy, though it contains a lot of prophetic writings. The Bible is primarily God speaking to us.

> All Scripture is God-breathed and is useful for teaching, rebuking, correcting and training in righteousness.
>
> —2 Timothy 3:16

"All scripture is God-breathed" means they come from the inspiration of God. They are useful and relevant for us. They teach us, rebuke us, correct us, and train us in righteousness. Righteousness is the essence of Christianity. The Greek word (*dikaiosune*) translated as righteousness here is the same word found in Romans 14:17: "For the kingdom of God is not a matter of eating and drinking, but of righteousness, peace and joy in the Holy Spirit." Righteousness is the essence of God's kingdom. If you want to hear God, you must begin by knowing what he has said. In hearing God you always go from the known to the unknown. For example, if you are asking God's direction about whom to marry, it is wise to find out first what he already said in his Word about who you can or cannot marry. Even though that will not tell you whether the person is Jane or Elizabeth, it is a good start. The Word of God is the known will of God. If you continue to ignore what God has already said to you through his Word, why would he tell you something new? That is one of the major problems of people who overemphasize different methods of hearing God — they always do it at the expense of the Word of God.

God's Voice Does Not Contradict His Word

One of the miracles of the Bible is the consistency of its message. The Bible consists of sixty-six books written by forty different authors over a period of about 1,800 years. Most of these authors did not know one another, and neither were most of them aware of each other's writing. Yet the message is amazingly consistent. This is the greatest proof that though it was written through forty different authors, the real author is God himself. We know that one attribute of God is his consistency; he is the same yesterday, today, and forever (see Hebrews 13:8). He does not make mistakes or have a need to correct himself. He does not and cannot improve or grow wiser. That is why when he speaks he does not contradict himself.

The point of this is to let you know that even now God cannot and does not contradict himself. Regardless of how he speaks to you today, whatever he says cannot be contradictory to what he has said before in his Word. How often does it happen that people will claim to have received a revelation or vision or voice from God about something and when you judge it carefully with the Word of God you find out that it contradicts it? This is due to complete ignorance of who God is and how he operates. A lot of this happens as a result of too much emphasis on these "spiritual methods" of God speaking to people. This tends to disregard the fact that God does not contradict himself. Let's take a look at a very interesting passage in the book written by the great Apostle Peter, which confirms this fact in a very powerful way:

> For we have not followed cunningly devised fables, when we made known unto you the power and coming

of our Lord Jesus Christ, but were eyewitnesses of his majesty. For he received from God the Father honour and glory, when there came such a voice to him from the excellent glory, This is my beloved Son, in whom I am well pleased. And this voice which came from heaven we heard, when we were with him in the holy mount. We have also a more sure word of prophecy; whereunto ye do well that ye take heed, as unto a light that shineth in a dark place, until the day dawn, and the day star arise in your hearts: Knowing this first, that no prophecy of the scripture is of any private interpretation."

—2 Peter 1:16–20 KJV

If you read this passage carefully, you will find out that Apostle Peter was speaking to the churches in general about the validity of the gospel of our Lord Jesus Christ. Here he tells them, "Look, this is not fable or story to us, we saw it with our very eyes. We were with him on the mountain when a voice told us that this is the Christ." He was making reference here to the transfiguration experience in Luke 9:1–36. The most powerful truth in the passage, however, is how he concluded it. What he essentially said is that as real as the transfiguration experience was to them, there is something more real and more trustworthy, and it is the account of the Old Testament about Jesus. In verse 19 he said, "We have also a more sure word of prophecy." Yes, transfiguration was real, but the Old Testament prophecies about Christ are even more real and reliable. I think that is a powerful truth.

Let me ask you, is there any vision or dream or revelation anyone can claim to have that is greater that the disciples' transfiguration experience? Yet compared with Old Testament writing, Peter said, "I would rather take the scripture than my subjective experience." I wish many believers today could see things the way Apostle Peter did. God has never contradicted himself, and he would not do it with anyone now.

God Often Confirms His Word in More than One Way

There is another principle that is very relevant when it comes to hearing God; it is the fact that God often speaks to us about an issue in more than one way. In other words, when he speaks he will confirm his word to us in another way. This principle actually reverberates throughout the Scriptures. He spoke to Abraham about the promise of the child multiples times; he showed himself to Moses many times; he also called Samuel three times before Samuel knew it was God. Even though it appears in many of these cases that it was due to faithlessness or ignorance of the people concerned, their behaviors and reactions actually characterize many of us in real life. It is typical for us as humans to be unsure of God's voice the first time he speaks; hence he will always find other ways to speak to us. Many times he will actually confirm his word to us using other people. Apostle Paul also says:

> By the mouth of two or three witnesses every word shall be established.
>
> —2 Corinthians 13:1 NKJV

Even when it comes to prophecy, Apostle Paul told the Corinthian church to let two or three prophets speak and also to let others weigh carefully what is said. This means that even prophecy needs to be confirmed by others using other means. It is important to understand that there is no method of hearing God that can stand by itself. It is humility to recognize that even the best of us is still human and is susceptible to error and deception. Failure to recognize this is called pride and can lead to costly error and destruction.

> Two or three prophets should speak, and the others should weigh carefully what is said.
>
> —1 Corinthians 14:29

This is not in any way to encourage indecisiveness and living in doubt; it is to discourage presumptuous attitude when it comes to hearing God.

Peace Is the Umpire of God's Will

When God speaks to you it produces faith—not fear, not doubt, and not confusion. "For God is not a God of confusion, but of peace" (1 Corinthians 14:33 ASV). The opposite of confusion is peace. You have an inner peace that God is your Abba, your Father. You received this peace when the Spirit testified and witnessed to your spirit that you were a child of God. The voice of the Spirit sounds like peace!

And let the peace (soul harmony which comes) from Christ rule (act as umpire continually) in your hearts [deciding and settling with finality all questions that arise in your minds.]

—Colossians 3:15 AMP

Peace is your umpire of God's will. In a baseball game, an umpire is a person appointed to rule on plays. In a typical baseball game there are a lot of voices, screams, and shouts from players, parents, and coaches all giving their opinions. At the end of the day, the final word comes from the umpire. An umpire is also a person appointed to settle a dispute that mediators have been unable to resolve—an arbitrator. Peace is the fruit of the Spirit meant to guide you in the matter related to God's will.

You will go out in joy and be led forth in peace; the mountains and hills will burst into song before you, and all the trees of the field will clap their hands.

—Isaiah 55:12

You will be led forth in peace. If there is no peace, then you are not led by God. No matter how rational and logically sound a decision is, it is important to always be sure you have the peace of God deep within you.

Who led them through the depths? Like a horse in open country, they did not stumble; like cattle that go down to the plain, they were given rest by the Spirit of the Lord. This is how you guided your people to make for yourself a glorious name.

—Isaiah 63:13–14

Isaiah clearly tells us how God guided his people. How did he guide them? He guided them when they were given rest by the Spirit of the Lord. *Rest* is another word for peace. This is the method God used to guide his people. God still uses this method today. The peace of God is what gives finality to our request; until peace comes, the prayer is not complete. Apostle Paul tells us that every request to God must end up in the peace of God that transcends all understanding.

Do not be anxious about anything, but in every situation, by prayer and petition, with thanksgiving, present your requests to God. 7 And the peace of God, which transcends all understanding, will guard your hearts and your minds in Christ Jesus.

—Philippians 4:6–7

The peace of God is not the peace based on logic but as a result of a heart surrendered to God in prayer until it finds itself in the midst of God's will. Every true prayer, though it may not start in the will of God, always ends in the will of God. Jesus started his prayer in the Garden of Gethsemane by saying, "If you are willing, take this cup from me," but he ended up with, "Not my will, but yours be done" (Luke 22:42). That is the nature of every true prayer: it always ends with us in the will of God with the peace of God that passes understanding.

Chapter 10

Final Destination

Do not let your hearts be troubled. You believe in God;
believe also in me. My Father's house has many rooms;
if that were not so, would I have told you that I am
going there to prepare a place for you? And if I go and
prepare a place for you, I will come back and take you
to be with me that you also may be where I am.
                                                    — John 14:1–3

One thing is clear; without a destination in mind there will
be no need for GPS. In our walk with God, while there
are many intermediary destinations, it will be unwise to not
talk about our ultimate destination. As believers in Christ Jesus
our ultimate destination is heaven. It is that of a life spent in
eternity with God. That is the final destination of every believer
in Christ Jesus. The Bible describes heaven as the beautiful place
that we go after we leave this world, where there is no more
pain, no more crying, and no more death (Revelation 21:4).
It is the place where God lives. Hell, on the other hand, is an
awful place and the final destination of those who reject Jesus
as their Savior. The Bible describes hell as a place of eternal,
fiery punishment. That's a reason to be saved!

The Bible is unmistaken about the fact that we are only in
this world temporarily. Every destination we have talked about
so far in this book is at best intermediary. They are more like
stopovers or rest areas on your way to the final destination.
You will understand this concept better if you have ever done
a cross-country trip. If you are a good planner, when you plan

your trip you also plan the stopovers. Your stopovers are places you stop along the way to rest or to catch some fun. They are part of the journey and all combine to add to the journey experience. You might stop over in a place because you have a friend or family there; it may be because there is something unique or historic about the place or simply to rest or stretch. However, those stopovers are only meaningful in the light of your final destination. Without the final destination, they are irrelevant and wouldn't have been in the picture at all. I want us to take a look at what the Bible says concerning this:

> If only for this life we have hope in Christ, we are of all people most to be pitied.
>
> —1 Corinthians 15:19

What a powerful statement! We have talked about all the beautiful things that we have in Christ Jesus, however if everything we have in Christ is limited to this earth, the scripture says we are to be pitied more than all men. The King James Version of the Bible says, "We are of all men most miserable." Hence in Christ Jesus, the ultimate hope is not in this life but after this life. The greatest benefit of a life spent with Christ here on earth is that of a life spent eternally with him in heaven. We must never forget that all the benefits of GPS we have mentioned throughout this book—purpose, prosperity, peace, and other good things God has in store for us—are only relevant in the light of our eternal destination, which is heaven.

The Greatest Hope Is Resurrection

Chapter 15 of 1 Corinthians is a response to questions and doubts about resurrection among the Corinthian church. Apostle Paul responds to these questions powerfully and adequately: Resurrection is the greatest promise we have in Christ Jesus. It is the greatest hope for a believer in Christ Jesus. It is the greatest right for every wrong done to man and the greatest comfort for every trouble our soul is subjected to. It is the ultimate victory over death and the chief of every promise God ever made. Here is another statement from 1 Corinthians:

But if it is preached that Christ has been raised from the dead, how can some of you say that there is no resurrection of the dead? If there is no resurrection of the dead, then not even Christ has been raised. And if Christ has not been raised, our preaching is useless and so is your faith.

—1 Corinthians 15:12–14

Our faith in Christ is useless without the resurrection of Christ, and it is the resurrection of Christ that guarantees our own resurrection. Resurrection guarantees that all does not end here after death. In comforting the Thessalonian church, apparently after the death of some believers among them, Apostle Paul went on to give us some insight about resurrection:

Brothers and sisters, we do not want you to be uninformed about those who sleep in death, so that you do not grieve like the rest of mankind, who have no hope. For we believe that Jesus died and rose again, and so we believe that God will bring with Jesus those who have fallen asleep in him. According to the Lord's word, we tell you that we who are still alive, who are left until the coming of the Lord, will certainly not precede those who have fallen asleep. For the Lord himself will come down from heaven, with a loud command, with the voice of the archangel and with the trumpet call of God, and the dead in Christ will rise first. After that, we who are still alive and are left will be caught up together with them in the clouds to meet the Lord in the air. And so we will be with the Lord forever. Therefore encourage one another with these words.

—1 Thessalonians 4:13–18

The period following the death, especially of a believer, can be the most traumatic and faith-trying period for the rest of the believers. This period is always characterized with questions, self-doubt, and bewilderment about God's word and promises. What the apostle is saying here is that the whole process is a result of ignorance about resurrection and that in the light of resurrection all the questionings and the bewilderments become moot. The hope of resurrection is the greatest comfort Apostle Paul offered the Thessalonian church and it is still the greatest comfort we all have now.

We Are Ambassadors Here on Earth

Another powerful truth the scripture provides is that of our status here on earth. Though now a United States citizen, as someone who migrated from another country, the word *status* is a very meaningful word to me, as it is for most immigrants. If you are an immigrant in the United States, your visa status determines many things about you: what you are able to do, whether you are able to work or not, the kinds of job you can do, what benefits you are qualified for, etc. As believers in Christ Jesus we must also be aware of our status here on earth. We are noncitizen residents of the earth.

But our citizenship is in heaven. And we eagerly await a Savior from there, the Lord Jesus Christ.

—Philippians 3:20

If we are not citizens of the earth, what kind of status do we then have? According to the Bible we are here on earth with a diplomatic visa status. I have met a few people who live in the United States but work for the consulate office of the country they are citizens of. I have also met people who work for organizations like the United Nations. These people have a special diplomatic visa status that gives them the right to live and work in the United States. The status also gives them many other enviable privileges as well. While they usually have a lot of juicy rights and privileges, the fact is, they are not citizens of the United States of America and have limited rights and privileges available to U.S. citizens. This is how the Bible describes our status as believers:

We are therefore Christ's ambassadors, as though God were making his appeal through us. We implore you on Christ's behalf: Be reconciled to God.

—2 Corinthians 5:20

We are ambassadors here on earth. An ambassador is the highest ranking diplomat who represents a nation and is usually accredited to a foreign sovereign or government. One thing is clear: An ambassador is not a citizen of the place he lives and works. He is a citizen of the country he represents. He is only in the foreign country on a temporary assignment and at some point he will be recalled back home. So is our status here on earth; we are here as Christ's ambassadors. We cannot afford to be too attached to the world; the Bible says that though we live in the world, we are not of the world (see 2 Corinthians 10:3). For example, it would be unwise for an ambassador to keep his most important investments in the foreign land, because he is only there temporarily and can be recalled at any time. He is better off putting his most important investments in his home country. In the same way, Jesus challenged us not to keep our investments here on earth, because it is not safe here.

But store up for yourselves treasures in heaven, where moths and vermin do not destroy, and where thieves do not break in and steal.

—Matthew 6:20

As an ambassador, no matter how much you enjoy the foreign country, you never forget that you are a foreigner there and you are there temporarily on an assignment. In fact, in many cases there are legal limits to what you can and cannot do in the foreign country. Also, because the bulk of your investments, your families, and interest are still in the home country, your mind is always there. In the same manner, believers are challenged to set our minds on thing above and not on earthly things.

Set your minds on things above, not on earthly things.

—Colossians 3:2

An ambassador's role in the country of service is only important relative to the country he represents. When he speaks on any matter, he does not speak his opinion but the opinion of the one he represents. He lives his life and conducts his affairs based on the instructions from the home country. So are we here on earth; we live our lives with an understanding that we represent our country of citizenship, which is heaven. We do not conduct our affairs based on our personal opinion, we only present the opinion of heaven, our home country. Also, we recognize that even if our GPS can get us to a lot of great places here on earth, it will be pointless and worthless if it can't get us to heavenly home, which is our final destination.

Jesus Is Coming to Take Us There

Toward the end of his ministry here on earth Jesus told his disciples (and also us) about our final destination and his plan to take us there. He said:

Do not let your hearts be troubled. You believe in God; believe also in me. My Father's house has many rooms; if that were not so, would I have told you that I am going there to prepare a place for you? And if I go and prepare a place for you, I will come back and take you to be with me that you also may be where I am.

—John 14:1–3

One of the reasons Jesus went back to heaven after his resurrection is to prepare a place for us there. After the preparation he is also coming back to take us to our final destination. At his ascension, after Jesus was taken up to heaven in the very eyes of the disciples, and as they continued to gaze at the sky, two angels appeared to them and repeated this powerful promise of his return.

"Men of Galilee," they said, "why do you stand here looking into the sky? This same Jesus, who has been taken from you into heaven, will come back in the same way you have seen him go into heaven."

— Acts 1:11

This anticipated experience is commonly referred to by believers as the rapture. It is the same promise Apostle Paul repeated to the Thessalonian church.

For the Lord himself will come down from heaven, with a loud command, with the voice of the archangel and with the trumpet call of God, and the dead in Christ will rise first. After that, we who are still alive and are left will be caught up together with them in the clouds to meet the Lord in the air. And so we will be with the Lord forever.

— 1 Thessalonians 4:16–17

Jesus is coming back to take us with him so we can be with him forever in heaven, where there will be no more pain, no more tears, no more sickness and disease, no more mourning or crying, and no more death. It is a place of eternal joy and ultimate fulfillment, and the final destination of the Christian journey here on earth. Apostle John was a man who saw the clearest glimpse of heaven that we know in the Scriptures today. In his epistle he describes what should be the attitude of anyone who has the hope of heaven when he says:

All who have this hope in him purify themselves, just as he is pure.

— 1 John 3:3

Anyone who has the revelation and a hope of heaven would not want to miss it for anything. There is nothing the world can offer you to compromise your desire for it. With this hope burning in our hearts, we must say no to ungodliness and worldly passions and pursue holiness and purity so that nothing will be able to stand in our way to our final destination.

CPSIA information can be obtained at www.ICGtesting.com
Printed in the USA
BVOW030438280113

311655BV00003B/8/P